LOGO designed by Michael Shifflett
Purchase & visit his incredible digital art at sieren.pixels.com

Cover Photo: an undocumented canyon in SW Utah

(Contact me at **BrettJ2002@gmail.com**)

Table of Contents

Thanks & Acknowledgements

"This book is the realization of a years-long dream made possible by the incredible support, encouragement, and inspiration of so many people. My passion for canyoneering runs deep, and my goal has always been to share this amazing sport with others.

Frustrated by the lack of standardized, accessible resources, I began this project in 2019. After nearly five years of work—rewriting, trimming over 500 pages to 350, editing photos, and refining every detail—this book along with my website (canyoneering101.com), is finally a reality thanks to many.

First, thank you to my amazing wife, Sarah, whose unwavering love, and support have been my foundation throughout. Deep gratitude to Shane Burrows (www.climb-utah.com) and Tom Jones (www.canyoneeringUSA.com), who sparked my passion for canyoneering, and to Justin McFarland and Scott Nielsen for the countless hours of learning and growth on the Bogley.com forums in the early 2000s.

Special thanks to my family: Greg, Linda, Jayne, Matt, Jen, Sara, Brian, Brooke, Jeff, McKinley, Miles; Chris and River Allen; Emma and Liam Dalton; the Coleman family: Brian, Julie, Issac, Nathan, Michelle, Emily, Joe, Anna, and Eric; and my amazing friends: Jeff Guest; Ian Napper; Dave Lamb; Brian and Kevin Stubbs; Ethan Baham; Josh Oyler, Matt Meldrum, Chris and Erica Riplinger, Trevor Parker, Michael Shifflett, Ira Lewis, Rick Green; and many others.

To everyone who contributed—whether through encouragement, advice, or direct help—thank you!"
— Brett Johnson

- Learn all about the exciting world of Canyoneering!
- Discover the exact **canyoneering gear** you need!
- Learn how to move through a technical canyon through various **sequencing** techniques!
- See actual "**gear loadouts**" of what you might bring through a slot canyon!
- Learn the "essential" **canyoneering knots**
- Understand the **basics of Rappelling** and Ascending Ropes
- Understand how to "**rig an anchor**"
- Know the **terminology**
- Join a free **community forum** to introduce yourself, ask/answer questions and help others who are new to this growing sport!
- Discover gear companies that cater to Canyoneering
- Easily remember the website's name and share it with others who are **new to the sport**!

What is Canyoneering101.com?

Canyoneering—also known around the world as Canyoning, Gorging, or Kloofing—is an exhilarating, niche adventure sport that involves descending through rugged, narrow slot canyons using a mix of hiking, rappelling, climbing, and swimming. It's not just about adrenaline—it's about exploration, problem-solving, and witnessing these tucked-away places in nature in its most raw and remote form.

Over the past 25 years, I've caught the canyoneering "bug" and at times, it has become an obsession! In my opinion, canyoneering at its roots is only truly meaningful when it's **shared**. That passion led to the creation of this book and its companion website (www.canyoneering101.com) —a comprehensive, beginner-friendly resource that walks you through the essential skills, techniques, and realities of canyoneering.

Unlike other websites or books that barely scratch the surface, **this project is built to go deep**—offering detailed, step-by-step guidance for those just getting started. The online version is completely free, and the book version is designed to be your trail companion—something you can read on the way to a canyon, mark up, and reference while you master knots or refine your understanding of canyon theory.

Canyoneering isn't a one-size-fits-all sport. **Every canyon is different**. Conditions change. Anchors disappear. Plans fall apart. You need to be ready for anything. **That's why learning the fundamentals is non-negotiable**. You can't rely on just a few skills or hope that everything will go as planned.

There are no shortcuts in the slot canyon world.

Canyons are remote. There's no cell coverage, no easy way out, and no one coming to help if you're not prepared. What happens if someone in your group gets stuck on rappel? What if an anchor you planned to use is missing or unsafe? What if someone falls or is injured miles from the trailhead?

You need to know how to respond—not just in theory, but in real-world, high-stress situations. **Because in canyoneering, there's no room for a false sense of security.**

And here's the truth: the canyon doesn't care if you're a beginner. **That's why this guide exists**—to teach you what you need to know before you ever clip into a rope.

Social media has done wonders for showing off the beauty of canyoneering—but it's also **created a false sense of simplicity**. You'll see epic photos, drone shots, smiling faces… but rarely do you hear about the anchor failures, the unexpected swims, the injuries, the exhaustion, or the sheer mental game involved.

Some of those creators just want clicks, likes, or sponsorships—and that's fine—**but you deserve to know the full story**. Beginners can easily get the wrong idea and walk blindly into danger. My mission is to break through that sensationalism and give you the full picture—good, bad, and everything in between.

There's **no global canyoneering curriculum**. Each guiding company, Facebook group, and online community has their own way of teaching. Some are helpful. Some are not. Some experienced canyoneers are generous with their knowledge. Others hoard it, refuse to help, or ghost beginners out of fear, pride, or past frustrations.

The result? **Beginners end up teaching beginners**. And that's dangerous. It leads to accidents, injuries, and sometimes fatalities. Not because those new to the sport are careless—but **because the culture hasn't supported them with clear, structured education.**

I'm here to change that.

This guidebook and website feature over **36 modules** designed to walk you through canyoneering in a **structured, logical way**. It starts with the absolute basics—gear, safety, terminology—and progresses toward more advanced techniques and real-world scenarios. You'll learn the knots that matter most, how to evaluate conditions, and how to think critically inside the canyon.

If you stick with it, you'll go from unsure beginner to confident beginner canyoneer—with a solid foundation to keep you and your group safe.

And who knows? Maybe your passion for the sport will lead you to become a certified guide, start your own canyoneering business, or simply become the friend everyone trusts on the rope.

Canyoneering is not for everyone—and that's okay.

If you're not into long, sweaty hikes, swimming through potholes, or rappelling off cliffs... no worries. But if you are? If you're the kind of person who embraces challenge, loves to problem-solve, and thrives in the wild—then this sport can absolutely change your life.

Additionally, most technical canyons involve rappelling. **Rappelling is serious business**. It might look easy in a YouTube video, but the moment you're standing at the edge of a 200-foot drop, with just your gear and your training to rely on, you'll understand the gravity of what you're doing—literally and figuratively.

The goal here isn't to scare you. It's to prepare you.

This book and website were built with one goal in mind: **to create a truly accessible, standardized learning platform for beginners.** A place where everyone speaks the same language, ties the same knots, and prioritizes safety above all else.

Who cares about these canyons? They're irreplaceable. We only get so many of them. And if we want to keep exploring them safely and respectfully, we need to raise the standard together.

Thanks for reading—and welcome to the start of your canyoneering journey.

Let's do this the right way.

-Brett

The story of:

"How I fell in love with Slot Canyons"

My love for slot canyons began on a family trip to Utah's San Rafael Swell back in 1994. I was 10 years old when we hiked **Little Wild Horse Canyon**, and it completely blew my mind! Imagine a place where the walls are so close you can touch both at the same time, yet they stretch impossibly high like "stone skyscrapers". Every twist and turn felt like an impossible maze. That experience stuck with me—I couldn't stop thinking about it for weeks. It lit a fire inside me, the beginning of a lifelong desire to "see what's out there."

Not far from Little Wild Horse is **Goblin Valley**, which quickly became our go-to basecamp for spring trips. Back then, it was remote and quiet—a hidden gem. The hot showers at the campground felt like a luxury to me as a kid in the '90s (who doesn't love a good hot shower after a dusty day of exploring?). I loved the magic of discovering canyons, squeezing through tight spots, and feeling like I was walking through the pages of a fantasy novel.

Back in those days, Little Wild Horse wasn't on most people's radar. No crowds, no waiting in line, no Instagram influencers dangling selfie sticks. But the internet changed everything. Today, it's hard to find an open campsite without booking a year in advance. These once-hidden places are now being "loved to death." That's a conversation for another day—shoot me an email (**BrettJ2002@gmail.com**) if you want to dive into that topic.

Those early adventures with my mom and little brother Jeff led me to join the Boy Scouts, where my outdoor obsession grew even stronger. One day, our Scout leader told us about this epic hike in Zion National Park called "**The Subway**." I had already been to Zion and done the usual hikes, but this one involved rappelling and swimming through narrow canyons—at age 16, I was hooked!

Back then, we didn't have YouTube tutorials or Reddit threads to tell us what to expect. Google wasn't the all-knowing oracle it is now. Hiking meant, well, hiking. I didn't even think about climbing or ropes—those seemed like advanced adult stuff. **But this hike changed all that**. It was completely new, wild, and exciting. That day in the Subway was a game-changer—truly **life-changing**.

It amazed me: here we were in the sweltering Utah heat, yet deep inside this canyon flowed crystal-clear, cool water year-round. There were waterfalls, green mossy walls, and red rock cascades—like something out of a dream. And yes, it was challenging in areas, but that only made it better. I walked out of there knowing I needed more of this in my life.

Eventually, I learned that people had been exploring these canyons since the 1970s. They called it "Gorging" back then. South Africans say "Kloofing." Europeans call it "Canyoning." Me? I'm American— we call it "**Canyoneering**." Whatever the name, we're all united by a shared fascination: discovering and descending nature's hidden cracks, canyons, and hidden places.

In the early 2000s, I started searching online for more technical canyons in Utah and quickly realized there wasn't much out there. Sure, there were a few blog posts and websites that listed gear and vague advice—but nothing standardized and nothing in-depth.

Regardless, I dove in. I read everything I could get my hands on— books by Mike Kelsey, Steve Allen, *Freedom of the Hills*, and scoured every online forum I could find. I then learned there were different types of canyons, different obstacles, and no, they weren't all the same. The answer to most questions? "It depends." All of this was starting to click in my head.

One of the best early resources I found was a Yahoo group called "Canyons," though I didn't discover it until much later. But the big moment came in 1999 when I stumbled upon a site called www.Climb-Utah.com, run by Shane Burrows—known online simply as "Shane." That site felt like finding the holy grail. Suddenly, I had access to canyon beta I didn't even know existed. I joined his "Circle of Friends" program and soaked it all up. I owe Shane a huge thanks, and I'm not alone—his work has helped a lot of people get started safely.

By 2007, more and more canyoneering sites and forums had popped up, but a frustrating trend emerged—people posting photos of amazing "secret" canyons with zero intention of sharing locations or details. It felt like a weird flex: "Look where I went... but I'm not telling you where it is." That kind of gatekeeping didn't sit right with me.

At the same time, I noticed a disturbing lack of information about accidents, safety, and real-world canyoneering education. Many of the people I met were figuring it out on their own—or worse, relying on one "expert" in the group. I've been on trips where only one person really knew what they were doing, which is a dangerous situation when something goes wrong.

That's when I decided to do something about it.

In 2019, I created a website that offers everything I wish I had when I was starting out: clear, free, and accessible info on gear, safety, knots, planning, and the realities of the sport.

I'm not here to replace professional training or real-world experience—but I *am* here to help people build a strong foundation so they don't go in blind.

My goal is simple: to create a resource that helps new canyoneers start off safe, smart, and confident. Whether you're just curious or already hooked, you can point your friends to this website instead of explaining everything from scratch. And once they've got the basics, they can come back to you for more challenging canyon adventures.

This project—both the website and this book—is about creating a community. One where knowledge is shared, safety is prioritized, and everyone has a chance to enjoy this incredible sport without feeling like an outsider.

Thanks for reading this far. I truly hope this book and the website help you fall in love with canyoneering the same way I did—one canyon at a time.

-Brett

Unit 1: "The Basics"

Modules 1 - 17

This section does NOT yet dive into the specific Canyoneering gear or ropes, knots or canyoneering techniques. That is provided in "**Unit 2 – The Essentials**" section.

The Basics section will help you determine, if this inherently-dangerous sport (because it is! e.g. You are rappelling off of high places, among a few things!), is too complex and isn't something worth pursuing within your comfort levels. I would nudge you a bit and help you realize that essentially, as the adage goes, you are really "hiking with ropes".

Of course, it's more than just "hiking" and "ropes" though, but if you can hike and have a desire to face a fear (or two), rappel (on your own!) into the depths of a canyon - than you can do this! But I'm also not trying to persuade those who really don't want to – to do it! There are things that CAN go wrong. Life-threatening even!

That's okay! I'm not offended! Or maybe, just maybe, you will be bit by the "bug" and want to consume all that you! That happens to most of us who discover this sport and want to absorb as much information as we can!

Canyoneering isn't just dropping into any random canyon at any given time and guarantee that you are going to be okay. After reading through this section, it will provide a simple answer of - it "**all depends**" on the canyon!

Sometimes variety is good (and adds to the "spice of life") and those "mediocre" canyons will add new experiences and allow you to be more comfortable on the ropes, make you more competent at rappels, and help you solidify skills.

Some of those 2-star rating canyons that you see on beta websites will often see very minimal people and provide you with an appreciation for all canyons later on. The "best" isn't necessarily the "best" all the time. It's okay that your "best" canyon is not everyone else's favorite!

We all like different things and for different reasons. Some want the challenge from the toughest of all canyons! Others seek the aesthetics or visual of the canyon only and care less about the technical aspects. Some want a good night stay in a hotel after a canyon, versus camping for 2-3 days in the hot desert with no amenities nearby. Etc.

But you know what? That's the great thing about this sport - you get to decide what and where you want to go and how you want to descend these slot canyons.

With that said, Canyoneering takes serious consideration with planning and forethought! Some canyons are great for beginners and other canyons would seriously injure or be lethal to the ill-prepared!

People have died by underestimating the canyon, by not doing their research and planning with not knowing the serious/lethal risks of that canyon. Sometimes, people will even ignore weather/rain warnings and decide to rappel into a canyon anyway.

Remember, a canyon is literally Mother Nature's sewer system! Live another day! **The canyon(s) will always be there! You will not!**

Some people and websites think that once you learn how to tie just a few knots, you are good to go! Very wrong! While you may get through some simple technical canyons, that doesn't mean that you were "successful". In other words, you got lucky! But maybe not next time! Do not take your safety and the safety of others for granted.

The purpose of these modules is to provide the context of the dangers and cautions found within the sport.

What is Canyoneering?

Module 1

Imagine a trail in Zion National Park, Utah, where summer temperatures soar past 100°F, yet deep within a slot canyon lies a year-round stream. Freshwater pools fed by springs and seeps offer a refreshing oasis—a stunning contrast to the surrounding summer desert heat! Canyoneering allows you to experience the awe of this hidden oasis!

These photos showcase the renowned "Subway" hike in Zion National Park, one of the most sought-after trails alongside Angels Landing.

Due to its popularity, amplified by social media, the park now requires a lottery permit system to preserve its pristine backcountry feel for this 10-mile adventure.

This training aims to equip you with enough knowledge to seek professional guidance from local canyoneering outfitters.

While this website offers valuable insights, it's not a substitute for professional instruction.

Canyoneering has its own culture—unwritten rules, "secret handshakes" for hidden canyons, and online trip reports where we share stories, mishaps, and lessons learned.

Keep in mind that canyoneering is inherently risky. Once you commit to a rappel and pull your rope, there's no turning back.

These canyons demand confidence, preparation, and the determination to see the journey through to the end.

It is NOT enough for ONE person to know how to tie all the knots or defeat obstacles. **EVERYONE** in your group must know these too.

More Than "Hiking with Ropes": Explore hidden secrets in slot canyons beneath deserts and forests.

Adventure Awaits: Descend cliffs, rappel heights up to 600 feet, and swim through canyon pools (although, sometimes it is less glamorous than it sounds)!

Inspired by Curiosity: Wondered what lies beyond a canyon drop-off or narrow trail? Canyoneering lets you find out.

The Ultimate Challenge: Thrilling, unforgiving at times, and perfect for those ready to solve its mysteries.

Start Here: Begin your canyoneering journey at the ultimate place for canyoneering beginners.

Your Safety!

Module 2

I will state this again and again throughout this book/website, these are the three golden canyoneering rules:

#1 - Safety First – Your safety along with everyone else, is the top priority.

#2 - Enjoyment – Have an incredible time! (Otherwise, why do it?)

#3 - Follow the Order – Always stick to rules 1 and 2, in that exact order.

Safety First: Your top priority is the safety of yourself and your group. Every decision should prioritize the team's safety and well-being.

Team Effort: Canyoneering is a team sport, not an individual one. Ensure everyone is equipped with the proper gear, knows key skills, and can perform basic canyoneering tasks (like knot-tying).

Don't Go Alone: Always go with experienced canyoneers—solo adventures are dangerous.

Weather Awareness: Canyons are shaped by water, and rain can create dangerous conditions. Avoid canyons if rain is expected.

Planning and Redundancy: Learn from others' experiences, plan ahead, and prepare for emergencies. Accidents can happen, but preparation reduces risk.

Preparation is Key: Don't be scared off—plan thoroughly, choose the right group, and ensure everyone is ready for the challenges ahead.

Canyoneering is indeed a thrilling sport, but accidents can and do happen. To prevent accidents in your group, it is essential to learn from past experiences of others and to be better prepared for the future. Planning and redundancy are critical factors that can help avoid accidents. Learning how to tie specific knots and how to react in emergencies are skills that can be learned and will help you feel more confident and safer. But it's never guaranteed. I wish it was, but it is not. You must take it seriously.

Finally, I encourage you not to let any websites scare you away from canyoneering altogether. Instead, use the information I am providing to plan your adventure better, invite specific friends and family who can match the canyon description and have the necessary endurance. (Don't bring little Tim who is eight-years old on a 12-mile slot canyon who has never rappelled before). With the right preparation and a focus on safety, you can have a fantastic time canyoneering while minimizing the risk of accidents.

In the following paragraphs, I listed some actual disasters and fatalities within the sport across the decades. You can use a search engine and search for these articles for further reading and pondering:

 "*I can't believe I survived*; video of flash flood crashing down on canyoneers" from StGeorgeUtah.com

"*Kolob Canyon Disaster*" from Climb-Utah.com

"*Flash Flood in the Black Hole*" from Climb-Utah.com

"*Flash Flood in Little Wild Horse Canyon*" from Climb-Utah.com

"*Special Report: The Keyhole 7*" from OutsideOnline.com

"*Surviving a Flash Flood in a Slot Canyon*" from OutsideOnline.com

Additionally, the following website was created by canyoneer Bob Allan and is a pretty comprehensive list of canyoneering-related accidents & fatalities:

https://www.smilingcricket.com/2019/04/the-death-thread.html

Please, learn from their mistakes, otherwise we are doomed to repeat them!

Objectivity & A Word of Caution!

Module 3

Be Objective: Make informed decisions by researching risks, challenges, group dynamics, gear, and weather. Scrutinize information sources for accuracy.

Double-Check Everything: Always question and inspect rigging and anchors—yours or others—for safety.

Speak Up: Trust your instincts. If something feels off, address it; your group's safety depends on collaboration.

Teamwork is Key: In the canyon, your group is your lifeline. Work together to face challenges and return safely.

"Proceed at your Own Risk", indeed.

Weather & Slot Canyons

Module 4

Weather is a major factor to consider when canyoneering! Probably one of the easiest and safest things that anyone can do - is check the weather for rain in the forecast. It's best said - don't go, even with a chance of rain. (1% chance means that 1% of the area is getting 100% of rain!)

Everyone should visit Weather.gov (created by National Oceanic And Atmosphere Administration/NOAA) -> "Forecast" -> "Local" and type in your destination area/closest city (not the canyon name) to get reliable 7-day pinpoint forecast, including temperatures of HIGHs and LOs, wind speed and direction, and precipitation estimate at that location and elevation for each of those 7 days.

Plan your trip on the "ideal" day. Remember "ideal' doesn't mean that rain is in the forecast! That should be one of the easiest decisions of your trip.

Do this a week prior, 3 days before, 2 days before, 1 day before, and the day off. Yes, the weather can change that quickly!

If anyone ever asks you how to get the weather for a slot canyon – always reference them here. This should be community practice and standard. Guiding companies use this same approach too. We are all on the same page now.

For advanced weather seekers, you can use another free tool at https://www.nhc.noaa.gov/satellite.php to look at "Water Vapor" in a certain area. This will give you context of where water is moving in the atmosphere. He uses Infrared Red to monitor Water Vapor, as it is a greenhouse gas. Viewing this gives a bigger picture of the storm speed, direction, and intensity. Very visual and clearly to see.

To use, select your "Region" and then click on the "Water Vapor" link.

Another webservice may be of assistance when planning when you are canyoneering in Utah: https://kutv.com/weather/radar

Flash Flood Risks

Check the Weather: Always check the forecast for rain.

Flash Flood Risks: Most common during summer monsoon (June–September), flash floods can develop rapidly, with water levels rising within minutes.

Flash Flood Warning Signs:
- Rapidly Rising Water
- Heavy rainfall
- Rushing water
- Debris (branches, leaves) in waterways
- Severe weather reports in area (if you have cell coverage)

Canyon Watershed & Flashflood Assessment:
Remember the 5 S's:
- **Size** – How large is the overall watershed feeding into the canyon?
- **Shape** – Is it long and narrow, potentially affected by storms far upstream? Or is it short but with many side drainages that can quickly fill during rain?
- **Surface** – What type of terrain will the rain fall on—pine needles, sand, sandstone, clay? Some surfaces absorb water, while others shed it quickly.
- **Saturation** – What's the current ground condition? Even sandy areas can flood if already soaked. Dry ground can also repel water, increasing runoff. Burn scars are especially hazardous.
- **Safety** – Are there safe zones like high ground or exits along the route? How frequent and accessible are they? Know if there's a point of no return.

Remember: Flash floods can be life-threatening. Stay alert and cautious.

Temperature Risks

Extreme Conditions:
- **Summer**: Desert temps can exceed 100°F (37°C), leading to heat exhaustion and dehydration.
- **Winter**: Temps can drop below 32°F (0°C), with ice or snow blocking paths and anchors.

Preparation Tips:
- Start with "ideal" conditions as a beginner.
- Always carry enough water and a filter for the entire trip.
- Be prepared for unexpected obstacles, like building anchors in snow or ice.
- Dehydration is a VERY serious issue and can make a person take "puzzling" suggestions or actions. Be aware of strange behaviors in judgement and address immediately!

Risks: Heat exhaustion, dehydration, and running out of daylight. Plan accordingly!

Waterflow Risks

Dangers of Flowing Water:
- Limits visibility, drowns out voices, and can push gear and people.
- High water flow can lead to immobilization or drowning scenarios.
- Flash floods can occur unexpectedly, with water levels rising within minutes or seconds.
- Floods can reach heights of 12 feet or more!

Key Safety Tips:
- Always check weather and flash flood forecasts before your trip.
- A "30% chance of rain" means 30% of the area could see measurable rain, not just a slim likelihood.
- Continuously evaluate weather and seek high ground immediately if conditions worsen.
- Wait for water levels to drop—usually within 24 hours—before proceeding.

Preparation and vigilance are key to staying safe!

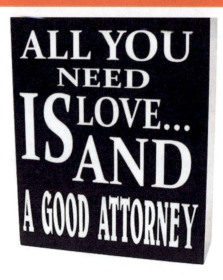

Canyoneering is **inherently dangerous** and requires extensive knowledge, equipment, and problem-solving skills. While this training provides general information, it is not a substitute for professional instruction or hands-on experience.

Canyons are unpredictable, with risks such as flash floods, injuries, hypothermia, heat exhaustion, uncontrolled rappelling speed or anchor failures. Always prioritize safety, exercise caution, and ensure your group is prepared. Rescue may be hours away and with no cell coverage.

Canyoneering101.com, Canyoneering101 LLC, and its owner, Brett Johnson, are not liable for injuries or fatalities resulting from the use of this information. You and your group assume and accept all risks and responsibility for you and your group's safety.

Canyoneering Ethics

Module 6

DO!

- Leave Only Footprints, Take Only Photos to preserve the environment.
- Leave an Emergency Note (**Module 35**) in your vehicle with details of your plan.
- Help and Encourage Others—outdoor activities are team efforts.
- Wear a Helmet for safety.
- Bring Enough Food and Water (plus extra) for the day.
- Hike in Canyon drainages to avoid creating damaging social trails.
- Avoid Stepping on Cryptobiotic crust—it takes decades to recover.
- Carry a First-Aid Kit (**Module 33**) for emergencies.
- Bring a Bivy for unexpected overnight stays (8+ hour hikes).
- Use Clear Communication like "watch out below" instead of yelling "rope" at popular hiking areas to avoid language confusion.
- Let Faster Canyoneers Pass to avoid bottlenecks.
- Report Graffiti to protect the natural beauty of canyons.
- Stick together as a group, don't separate!

- **No** Pets in Technical Canyons—please take them to non-technical areas to avoid possible harm to the animal.
- **Avoid** Horseplay on rappel or near edges to prevent accidents.
- **Don't** Overestimate Your Abilities—be realistic about skills and risks.
- **No** Rope Bouncing when rappelling—it increases force on anchors and risks damage.
- **Don't** Create Rope Grooves—place anchors to avoid harming the rocks.
- Maintain quiet/respect in public areas—**avoid** loud talking or showing off near the public rappelling/hiking areas.
- Use Clear Communication—say "watch out below" instead of "rope!" in public areas. **Don't** just yell "rope". Most people have no idea what to expect when they hear the word "rope".
- **Don't** Block Faster Groups—let them pass to prevent bottlenecks.
- Respect Private Property— **do not** trespass. Trespassing risks access for everyone. Abusing the trust of landowners can cause the entire community to lose access to these areas forever.

"Take...Only Pictures."

"Leave...Only Footprints."

"Keep Nothing...But Memories."

"Leave No Trace" is a crucial ethos in the hiking, camping, and backpacking world. It means that we should leave the place we explored in better condition than we found it. This includes leaving no trash, using available bathrooms or digging holes for our needs.

Leaving no trace is essential because it helps preserve the natural environment and maintain the pristine state of the wilderness for future generations. It also helps us to connect with nature more authentically and experience it as it is, rather than as a human-altered landscape. the environment for future generations by minimizing human impact.

Leave it Better: Pack out all trash, use proper bathroom practices (such as pooping 200 feet away from water sources and packing it out (if in a narrow slot canyon), don't vandalize or spray-paint, and limit cairn building.

Preserve Nature: Protect the environment for future generations by minimizing human impact, become their stewards (as canyon's don't have a voice), and don't create new road paths to the trailhead or canyon.

Respect the Wild: As canyoneer Tom Jones once said about canyoneering, "This is not Disneyland"—nature is raw and should remain unaltered.

Avoid Excessive Cairns: They disturb habitats, create visual clutter, and mislead hikers. If you find unnecessary cairns, dismantle them responsibly.

Connect: Experience nature in its pure, no music (in my opinion) untouched state while helping preserve its beauty for years to come.

Do <u>NOT</u> do this!

Place your Rope in a better spot for when you retrieve your rappel rope so it doesn't drag (thus creating the <u>rope grooves</u> that you see below).

<u>Photo Credit</u>: Alan Giles (used with permission)
Leprechaun Canyon

Photo Credit: Sam Staten (used with permission)
Cassidy Arch Canyon

Photo Credit: Tyler Wangsgard (used with permission)
Unknown slot canyon

Canyoneering Terminology

Module 8

A glossary of the words or terminology that are commonly used, said, and made fun of in Canyoneering.

I've also added my opinion on some of the words, so you don't sound like a complete noob when you are among your fellow canyoneering comrades.

Abseil - A German word that literally means "down rope" ("ab" = down, "seil" = rope). Non-U.S. folks will use this term to do what people living in the United States call "rappelling". In other words, it means exactly the same thing as going down the rope.

Anchor - this is what we refer to where your rappel rope will be connecting to, e.g. a tree trunk, a large rock or boulder, a bolted anchor on the wall, or even a "meat anchor" which means using a person(s). Your rappelling weight (which also means force in this context) will all be held up by this "anchor". Sometimes you will hear the term "bomber anchor". It means that the anchor is installed properly and is going to hold a lot of weight/force. A "marginal" anchor is less than ideal one due to the lack of bolts or natural objects (tress, roots, rocks, sand, and water) in a canyon, or a flat out poorly installed anchor (and location).

Approach - this is the (hiking) path that you take from the trailhead to reach the literal slot-canyon portion. Some involve a 5-minute hike and others might take you 5 hours (or more) just to reach the canyon itself.

Ascend - to climb UP a rope. One must use a special system in order to climb a rope, in case you cannot retrieve your rappelling rope.

ATC - a famous descender/rappel device made by Black Diamond. The better version to use for canyoneering is the ATC-XP as it contains "teeth" which adds another "mode" to add friction while you rappel. They range between $20-30 and have their pros and cons. The canyoneering community doesn't suggest using an ATC-XP unless for the shortest of rappels (less than 50 feet) as one cannot add more friction while rappelling, and one cannot lock off the device.

ATS - a descender/rappel device made by Sterling.

Autoblock - a friction hitch tied with a loop of rope or webbing around the rappel rope and attached to the harness. It acts as a backup break while rappelling, allowing the canyoneer to stop automatically (but not guaranteed) if they let go of the rope. This knot provides an additional safety measure, especially useful on long rappels or in case of hand fatigue, as it slows or stops the descent if control is lost.

Belay - refers to a technique used to provide safety to a climber or canyoneer during a descent or ascent. It involves managing the rope to control the descent speed and prevent falls. The belayer uses a belay device to create friction on the rope, allowing them to catch a fall or control the descent. This technique is especially important during rappelling, where the belayer ensures the safety of the person descending by maintaining tension on the rope and being prepared to stop their fall if necessary. A "Fireman's belay" is this type of example.

Belay Loop - This loop is found on rappelling harnesses and is distinguishable by the off-color one from the other loops. This is the life-supporting loop where you attach yourself via a carabiner or load-bearing knot to the rappel device or P.A.S (Personal Anchor System) or safety tether.

Belayer - the title of the person performing the bottom-rope belay or top-rope belay.

Bend (rope) - in rope terminology, a "bend" is what is the correct name for when you want to join two ropes together via a knot. IE -

Double Fisherman Bend, Water Bend (if using two different strands of webbing).

Beta - the information that contains that always changing canyon conditions or route information. "Beta" in software terminology means that the software is changing and not complete. Or in other words, expect change. Likewise with canyoneering. If you read about a report of a group going down having an epic time, you may or may not experience the same thing. So go in prepared for changing conditions. Primarily when it comes to water in the canyon. There could be more or less. And that could make it easier or harder! That's why the term "beta" is used. The information is only accurate as the day it was published. To be fair though, beta providers do change their information if they hear anything from the community. But water levels and anchor conditions are the primary changing factors in canyoneering.

Bight (rope) - an "Old English" word with Germanic origin meaning "a bend or angle". In rope terminology, the curved section of the rope that is being tied into a knot. Commonly mistaken as a "loop".

Biner (same as Carabiner) - pronounced "bean-er" and is slang for the full-name of Carabiner. Canyoneers will use the two words: "biner" and "carabiner" interchangeably. There is no difference between except, the word "carabiner" has 4 syllables while "biner" has 2 so it's faster to say the latter.

Biner Block - an option of a static-block used for rigging a rappel. A carabiner is used in conjugation with a hitch knot, such as a clove hitch. A carabiner that is bigger than the quick link/rapide is a must.

Bivy (same as Bivouac/Bivy) - the English shortened word for Bivouac (pronounced "biv-oo-ack"). A French, low German word - "biwacht" meaning "by guard". In canyoneering, rock-climbing, or even hiking, to take a bivy means to take an unplanned or temporary camp. Sometimes in canyoneering, especially on canyons that involve 8+ hours, it is suggested to "plan for a bivy", meaning to bring an extremely light sleeping bag and tarp to sleep on in case plans take longer than expected. Some refer to an "emergency blanket" as a bivy, and indeed that it is what it is used for. You can buy more expensive (and more comfortable) as they offer complete protection from the elements and bugs) such as ones made by REI, Outdoor Research, and SOL. They range from $100 - $250 and that is essentially the "tent", but you would still need to buy the sleeping bag bivy in addition. You do not need a bivy for small canyon trips, but anything longer than 8+ hours it may be a good idea to bring one. Please do more research on bivy options before buying the first one that you see online. You do not want to carry excessive gear in your canyoneering bag.

Bolt - a fixed anchor that is drilled into rock. The two most common types of bolt types are "glue-ins" and "expansion". Just remember this safety note, just because you see a bolt in the rock doesn't mean that it is readily safe and usable. Remember to check every anchor, every trip, every time. If there is movement into the bolt when pulled on, DO NOT use it. Reevaluate anchor situation at that location and proceed. This is why we stress in that every canyoneer should bring 30+ft of webbing with them to every canyon.

Bolt Kit - a set of tools and hardware used to install permanent anchors in the rock for safe rappelling and climbing. It typically includes bolts, hangers, a drill (often a hand drill for remote locations), and other necessary tools. Bolt kits are used when natural anchors are insufficient, allowing canyoneers to create reliable anchor points. However, placing bolts is often considered a last resort and may be restricted in some areas to preserve the natural environment.

"Bolt Wars" - refer to conflicts within the community over the ethical use of bolts for anchors in canyons. Some canyoneers advocate for minimal or no bolting, aiming to preserve the natural environment and challenge themselves by using natural anchors. Others believe bolts are essential for safety, especially in high-traffic areas or challenging canyons where natural anchors may not be available.

These differing perspectives can lead to tensions, with some individuals adding bolts and others removing them. The term "bolt wars" reflects this ongoing debate over balancing safety, environmental impact, and the "purity" of the canyoneering experience.

Boulder - A large rock that can obstruct passage or provide potential climbing holds.

Brake hand - the hand that controls the descent speed while rappelling. By gripping and applying tension to the rope below the rappel device, the brake hand slows or stops the descent.

Bridging - this is a "canyon sequencing" technique used to traverse a slot canyon. See Module 29 - "Moving (Sequencing) in a Slot Canyon. One would place both hands on one wall of the canyon and their feet on the opposite and you would move by moving perpendicular to the canyon one appendage at a time.

Cairn - a small stack of rocks used as a marker to show the route or the location of an anchor. Cairns help guide canyoneers through complex terrain or indicate safe descent points.

Candition.com - a word that combines "condition" and "canyon" together in a memorable name. A free website that is crowd-sourced that allows canyoneers to post "conditions" on their recent canyon trip. They are brief reports on water and anchor conditions, and anything out of the ordinary to report so that anyone can get relevant information for trip planning. However, canyons can dry out quickly, anchors can be changed (or removed) with each passing party, or storms can pass and quickly refill the canyon water found in the canyon. Caution is highly recommended that you do not take each "candition" as your expectation. That is unwise and potentially dangerous. It is to be used to help assist or aid in canyon planning/research so that one can be aware of new hazards or issues that are found within the canyon.

Canyon - A deep, narrow valley with steep sides, often carved by water.

Canyoneer - a person who explores and descends canyons, often using techniques like hiking, scrambling, rappelling, and swimming to navigate challenging terrain.

Canyoneering - Canyoneering is the sport of exploring and descending canyons using a mix of hiking, climbing, rappelling, and swimming to navigate through rocky terrain, narrow slots, and waterfalls.

Carabiner - a strong, metal loop with a spring-loaded gate, used for connecting various components of the climbing or rappelling system. They play a crucial role in safely attaching ropes, harnesses, anchors, and other equipment. Each carabiner has a strength rating measured in kilonewtons, indicating how much force it can withstand before it fails. Proper selection, use, and regular inspection of carabiners are essential. As sand easily eats through aluminum carabiners, more and more canyoneers are opting for more expensive, heavier, but nearly sand-resistant *STEEL* carabiners.

Key types of carabiners include:
- **Locking Carabiners**: These feature a locking mechanism that prevents accidental opening, enhancing safety.
- **Non-locking Carabiners**: Simpler and lighter, these are used for quick connections where a lock isn't necessary.
- **Twist Lock**: great for Class C (flowing water). NOT great for SW America due to sand preventing consistent-closing and correct locking of gate.
- **Screw Gate**: your typical Carabiner style for SW America

Chimneying - this is a "canyon sequencing" technique used to traverse a slot canyon. See Module 29 - "Moving (Sequencing) in a Slot Canyon. In this technique, one places their hands against one wall and their back (or rear end) against the opposite wall. Rather than rappelling, one could "chimney" down a particular section using this method.

Chockstone - A rock that is wedged in a narrow part of the canyon, often creating a natural obstacle.

Colorado Plateau - in simplistic terms, a very large desert plateau that extends from parts of Utah, Colorado, Arizona and New Mexico. In Utah alone, there are over 650 documented slot canyons. In fact, some canyon obsessed folks, even relocate to Utah strictly for the canyoneering aspect alone! See Wikipedia.com for more information on the Colorado Plateau.

Contingency - refers to a planned response to potential emergencies or unexpected situations that may arise during a descent or traverse. This could include having backup gear, alternative routes for exit, or specific protocols for addressing injuries or equipment failure.

CRITR - a specialized rappelling device used in canyoneering that provides adjustable friction for controlled descents. Shaped like a figure-8 with additional features, it allows canyoneers to easily change friction mid-rappel, enhancing safety on long or variable descents.

Cryptobiotic Soil - delicate, living soil crust found in desert environments, made up of organisms like algae, fungi, and bacteria. It helps prevent erosion and supports plant life, so EVERYONE take care to avoid stepping on it to protect the fragile ecosystem, especially where water is scarce.

Crux - refers to the most difficult or technically challenging section of a canyon route. This could involve a particularly steep or tricky descent, a complex rappel, a challenging climb, or an obstacle that requires advanced skills to navigate. The crux is often the point that requires careful planning, skill, and sometimes specific gear (e.g. water anchor, sand trap) to overcome, making it a critical part of the planning process.

Descender Device (same as "Rappel Device") - is a piece of equipment specifically designed to control the descent of a canyoneer when rappelling. These devices create friction on the rope, allowing the user to manage their speed and safely descend vertical or steep surfaces. Examples include figure-eight, ATC, rappel rack, CRITR, SQUWREL, and more.

Double Strand - refers to a specific setup where two strands of rope (typically, from the same rope) are used for a rappel or to create an anchor. Imagine coming to a bolted anchor at a rappel and put one side of the rope through the rapide and the other side through the other. It does not need to be equal, however, they BOTH need to be touching the ground. Your descender device then attaches to BOTH strands in order to rappel. Otherwise, you rappel on one side of the rope but not the other making it unsafe. Many accidents have happened because of this, especially in the case of "biner blocks" where canyoneers attach the "pull-cord side" and not the "rappel side" of the rope.

DRT - stands for "Double Rope Technique." This method involves using two ropes—typically a main rappel rope and a pull cord or another rappel line—during descents.

Down-climb - a technique used in order to descend (or overcome) an obstacle in the canyon, that does NOT involve rappelling. Some people can down-climb sections in the canyon that others rappel. That comes from experience and skill-level. Just because you see bolts in a canyon, doesn't necessarily mean that you have to use them - especially for short rappelling canyons. See Module 29 - Moving (Sequencing) Through a Slot Canyon, for more information and pictures.

Drainage - refers to the water flow system within a canyon, including how rainwater and runoff are directed through the terrain. It encompasses the channels and paths that water takes, which can significantly influence the canyon's features, such as pools, waterfalls, and potholes.

Drop - A vertical section of a canyon that requires rappelling or climbing to descend safely.

Dynamic Rope - a type of rope designed to stretch under load, such as when it is used for rock-climbing and/or catching a fall. This stretch helps absorb the impact forces, reducing the risk of injury or equipment damage. Rock climbers use this rope exclusively, however, canyoneers typically use static ropes due their decreased size, easy ability to retrieve the rope after rappelling. See "static rope" for more information.

Egress (see "Ingress" for opposite) - refers to the process of exiting or escaping from a canyon. It involves planning and executing the route taken to leave the canyon safely, whether through a designated exit point, climbing out, or navigating back to the trailhead.

EDK (European Death Knot) - is a term used to describe a specific knot, also known as the Figure-Eight Follow-Through Knot. It is commonly used to connect two ropes of unequal or equal diameter together, such as the pull-cord to the rappel rope. However, I would NOT rappel on this but rather use it as a retrieving rope technique. The term "death knot" is somewhat misleading; it emphasizes the importance of proper tying and inspection because, if not tied correctly, it can lead to failure during a rappel or ascent. While the knot itself is strong and secure when properly executed, canyoneers must be vigilant in ensuring it is correctly tied.

Fireman Belay - see "belay" for additional information. This bottom-belay is the most common and can be performed by most able-body people. This is performed when the person is falling while on rappel, the "belayer" pulls down very firmly (and quickly!) the rappel rope to the ground. The mechanic of this is that it makes the rope taught (or tight) and prevents the rappel rope from feeding through the device stopping the out-of-control rappeler from continuing. Controlling how taught that rappel rope with the rappeler on it is how you would control their speed.

First-descent - this is a sought-after title within the Canyoneering Community. Canyons are still discovered/uncovered in this day and age, and you get the claim the "privilege" of descending it first.

Free Rappel (also called "Free Hang") - refers to a descent technique where the climber or canyoneer descends a vertical drop using a rope, but without being in contact with the rock face or using a controlled belay system. Instead, the individual is fully suspended and relies solely on the rope and their harness for support. While this type of rappel can be exhilarating, it also requires careful control of descent speed and awareness of the landing area to ensure your safety. Proper techniques are essential to perform a free rappel safely, such as dangling your backpack from your harness versus wearing it.

Ghosting - refers to the practice of leaving no trace of a descent or ascent in a canyon, particularly in terms of minimizing the visual and environmental impact. This includes avoiding the creation of permanent anchors or markings, cleaning up any gear or trash, and not disturbing the natural environment. The term can also describe a scenario where a canyoneer descends a route or area that is less traveled or known, often in a way that doesn't draw attention to their passage.

Hand-line - this is a "canyon sequencing" technique used to traverse a slot canyon. See Module 29 - "Moving (Sequencing) in a Slot Canyon. Used at short rappels (less than 10-feet in height), an option of using a handline may be suggested. Rather than putting on a harness and rappelling the short distance, one could hold onto the rope as tight as they can, and slowly slide down the rope or do a hand-over-hand descent on it. The caution is that they are not roped in, so the consequences are that they would fall if a slip was to happen. Sometimes a handline is used in areas where a person is down-climbing or up-climbing an obstacle and just need something to hold onto while they navigate the obstacle. Also, not everyone has the arm/muscle strength for a handline and have witnessed a few friends struggling and even slipping while using a handline.

Harness - a piece of safety equipment worn that secures the person to a rope system during rappelling or rock-climbing. The harness consists of a waist belt and leg loops, which are mostly adjustable for a secure fit. Often, it includes gear loops for attaching carabiners and other equipment.

Hitch (rope) - refers to a type of knot that is used to secure a rope to an object, such as an anchor point, or to attach two pieces of rope together. Hitches are typically adjustable and can be easily released under tension, making them useful in various scenarios. A popularly used hitch includes the "clove hitch" (or "triple clove").

Ingress (see "Egress" for opposite) - refers to the act of entering a canyon or a specific section of it. This includes the planning and execution of the approach to the canyon. Ingress involves considerations such as the chosen entry point, the terrain, and any potential obstacles or hazards that might be encountered.

Keeper Pothole - refers to a deep, water-filled hole in a canyon that can trap a person or an object. These potholes are often formed by the erosion of rock and can vary in size and depth. Keeper potholes are particularly dangerous because they may not be easily escapable, especially if the water is deep and the walls are steep or slippery. Knowing if the canyon you are descending contains one is a crucial part of the planning process. On the execution side, having a knowledgeable and able-body team to problem solve it must be done. Otherwise, you are literally stuck in the canyon. You won't be able to proceed onward.

Jenny West – her, along with RAM were the first ones to descend the iconic and infamous POE canyon in the 1980s, Choprock, and many other tough technical canyons before most people even thought about rappelling INTO a slot canyon.

kN (kilonewton) - is a unit of measurement used to quantify force, specifically in the context of load-bearing capacities of ropes, anchors, and other equipment. One kilonewton is equivalent to approximately 224.8 pounds of force. Ropes and carabiners are rated for specific kilonewton values, indicating the maximum force they can withstand before failure.

LDC (Left Down Canyon) - used to provide directional guidance, indicating that a route or feature is located to the left side as one descends (down) through the canyon.

LUC (Left Up Canyon) -used to provide directional guidance, indicating that a route or feature is located to the left side as one ascends (up) through the canyon.

Loop (rope) - refers to a section of rope that has been formed into a circular shape, often by tying the rope back on itself. Loops are commonly used in various applications, such as creating anchors, tying knots, or securing gear.

Monsoon Season - refers to the time of year, typically during the summer, when heavy rainstorms are more frequent, especially in desert regions. These storms can cause flash floods in canyons, making canyoneering dangerous and requiring extra caution.

Neoprene - type of synthetic rubber used to make wetsuits, neoprene booties and gloves.

Nylon - a strong, lightweight synthetic material commonly used for ropes, webbing, and harnesses. It is durable and resistant to abrasion, making it ideal for the rugged conditions of canyoneering.

Overhang - refers to a section of rock or cliff that extends outwards, creating a ledge or drop that is steeper than vertical. Overhangs can pose unique challenges during rappelling, as they can require specific techniques to safely navigate the descent. Descending an overhang may require special approaches, such as "swinging" away from the rock face to avoid getting stuck or using a technique called "free rappel."

Partner Assist - this is a "canyon sequencing" technique used to traverse a slot canyon. See Module 29 - "Moving (Sequencing) in a Slot Canyon. There are numerous techniques to bypass or overcome obstacles in a canyon, but anything that requires a second (or third or fourth) person, such as you stepping into their hands or on their shoulders would be classified as a "partner assist".

PAS (Personal Anchor System) - same meaning as Safety Tether.

Polyester - a strong, durable synthetic material often used for webbing and ropes. It is resistant to UV damage and abrasion, making it a good choice for gear exposed to harsh outdoor conditions.

Pothole - A deep, water-filled hole in a canyon, often requiring swimming or climbing to navigate.

Prusik - a type of knot or a loop of rope used as a backup for rappelling or climbing. It can be tied around the main rope, and when weight is applied, it tightens and provides extra security, helping to ascend or stop a rappel.

Pull-Cord - is a lightweight rope used to retrieve a rappel rope after completing a descent. It allows the canyoneer to pull the main rappel rope back up, ensuring that it is not left hanging in the canyon, which can prevent tangling or damage and facilitate faster descent of the canyon.

Quick Link (or Rapide) - a small, metal connector used to attach ropes to anchor points. It is a reliable, reusable alternative to knots, providing a secure connection that can be easily opened and closed with a screw-locking mechanism.

"RAM" – a nickname given to Steve Ramras. One of the original epic Utah explorers, similar to others like Mike Kelsey, Jenny West, Dennis Turville and Steve Allen . RAM started the then famous Yahoo.com Groups: Canyons were he shared many, many stories and adventures and beta to the canyon group. MANY canyon friendships were made because of him.

Rap - is a colloquial term for rappel/rappelling.

Rappel - refers to the technique of descending a vertical or steep surface using a rope. The canyoneer is secured to the rope via a harness and uses a rappel device to control their descent.

Rapide - refers to a type of quick-link or connector used to facilitate the attachment and detachment of gear in a rappel or climbing system.

It typically features a locking mechanism that ensures a secure connection.

Rappel Device (same as "descender device") - is a piece of equipment specifically designed to control the descent of a canyoneer when rappelling. These devices create friction on the rope, allowing the user to manage their speed and safely descend vertical or steep surfaces. Examples include figure-eight, ATC, rappel rack, CRITR, SQUWREL, and more.

RDC (Right Down Canyon) - used to provide directional guidance, indicating that a route or feature is located to the right side as one descends (down) through the canyon.

RUC (Right Up Canyon) - used to provide directional guidance, indicating that a route or feature is located to the right side as one ascends (up) through the canyon.

"Rich"/Rich Carlson - a well-known person in the canyoneering community, recognized for his contributions to the sport, particularly in the areas of developing canyoneering techniques, safety standards, and mapping canyons. He has written extensively on the subject and helped to popularize canyoneering in the United States, especially in regions like the Colorado Plateau. Started the American Canyoneering Association.

"Rig Releasable" - refers to the setup of a rappel or anchor system that allows for the rope or load to be released quickly and safely under certain conditions. This technique is particularly useful in situations where it's necessary to free the rope after a descent or to facilitate the quick escape of a canyoneer in an emergency. Rigging releasable systems adds an extra layer of safety and flexibility in canyoneering, enabling canyoneers to respond effectively to unexpected situations.

Rigging - refers to the process of setting up the canyoneering anchors for safe descents, ascents, and traverses within a canyon. This involves preparing anchors, ropes, and other gear to create a secure and reliable system for navigating rappels safely for yourself and groups behind you.

Safety Check - A pre-descent inspection of gear and setup to ensure all systems are secure.

Safety Tether - is a short length of rope or webbing used to connect a canyoneer to a secure point, such as an anchor or a harness, to enhance safety during technical maneuvers. The primary purpose of a safety tether is to provide additional security and prevent falls, especially in precarious situations like near edges, during rappels, or while navigating difficult terrain.

Sandtrap - a technique and tool used to create an anchor point when no bolted or natural anchors are available. It involves filling a strong, durable bag with sand, which is then placed near the rappel point to create a stable and reliable anchor for rappelling. Another rope is attached to the bag to release the sand and to retrieve the sandtrap and rappelling rope. This method is often used in desert environments where other options may be limited and is considered to be used by trained canyoneers as it is an advanced technique for harder technical canyons.

Scramble/Scrambling - A method of climbing using hands and feet on steep or rugged terrain.

"Send it" - a said expression that I loathe hearing when canyoneering. It originates from skiers and mountain-bikers when they were about to drop over the edge or about to do something "epic BRO!". In canyoneering, it's quite anticlimactic when you hear this phrase when someone is about to rappel and then takes 30 seconds for them to transition over the edge. In canyoneering, it's said in jest.

"Send it, Bro!" - a derivative of the above, but with the added word-enhancer "Bro!". Even said to women!

Sequencing - how one traverses through a slot canyon. Methods include walking, stemming, hand-lining, rappelling, chimneying, down-climbing, up-climbing, bridging, and using partner-assist techniques. See Module 29 for pictures of these methods.

Shane Burrows - founder of the website Climb-Utah.com, which is known for detailed beta called the "Circle of Friends". One of the first, online U.S. beta websites specific to canyoneering.

Sheath - the outer protective layer of the rope. It is typically made of braided fibers and serves to protect the inner core of the rope from abrasion, UV damage, and environmental wear. The sheath also provides the rope with flexibility and strength, ensuring it performs well during rappelling or climbing.

Sling - A loop of webbing or rope used to create anchors or to connect gear.

Slot Canyon - A narrow canyon characterized by vertical walls and often requiring technical skills to navigate. A narrower version of a "canyon".

SQWUREL - type of rappelling device used in canyoneering that combines the features of a friction device and a self-braking mechanism. It allows the user to control their descent with adjustable friction and can also act as a backup to prevent uncontrolled rappelling, improving safety on long or challenging descents.

Single-strand - refers to a single rope or line used for rappelling or climbing, as opposed to double or twin ropes. A single strand is typically used when conditions allow, but it requires careful attention to the rope's strength and wear, as it doesn't provide the redundancy of multiple ropes.

Slog - refers to a long, tiring, and often difficult section of the canyon that requires persistent effort to navigate. It usually involves challenging terrain, such as deep sand, mud, or steep slopes, making progress slow and exhausting.

SRT (Single-Rope Technique) - This method involves using a single rope for both ascending and descending rappels. You will attach a second rope to the anchor system/rigging so that you can retrieve your rappel rope once you finish the rappel.

Static Rope – a type of rope that does not stretch much under load. It is commonly used for rappelling, rigging, and other situations where minimal rope movement is needed. Static ropes provide more control and stability, but they do not absorb shock like dynamic ropes.

Stemming - this is a "canyon sequencing" technique used to traverse a slot canyon. See Module 29 - "Moving (Sequencing) in a Slot Canyon. In this technique, one places one hand and one foot on one side of the canyon wall, and the other hand and foot on the opposite wall. The one would move up or down-canyon in a forward direction by alternating move and feet movements to make forward progress.

Technora - a high-performance synthetic fiber used in some ropes. It is known for its exceptional strength, heat resistance, and durability, making it ideal for situations where ropes are exposed to abrasion, heat, or heavy use, such as during rappelling or navigating rugged canyons.

Toggle - refers to a small, often rigid piece of equipment used to secure or stabilize an anchor, such as in a sandtrap, watertrap, or totem. It helps ensure the anchor is strong and stable by preventing movement or slippage, allowing for a secure point to rappel or set up other equipment.

Tom Jones - known as the "emperor" of Canyoneering. Founder of 'Imlay Canyon Gear'. Founder of CanyoneeringUSA.com. Frequents CanyonCollective.com and Bogley.com commenting on all things Canyoneering.

Toss N' Go - refers to a technique used to set up a rappel where the canyoneer quickly tosses the rope down to the landing area without securing it to an anchor first. This method is typically employed in situations where the descent is straightforward and the canyoneer is confident in the setup. The primary advantage is speed; it allows the canyoneer to quickly get the rope down and begin the descent without taking extra time to secure the anchor initially. This technique is best used in scenarios where the landing area is safe, and there are minimal risks, such as falling debris or swift water. While toss and go can be a useful technique for experienced canyoneers, it requires careful consideration of safety and the specific conditions of the canyon to ensure a safe descent.

Trade Canyon - refers to a popular or well-established canyon route that is frequently visited and known for its relatively predictable and accessible features. These canyons are often documented and used as a benchmark for canyoneering.

Traverse - refers to moving horizontally across a section of a canyon, typically along a ledge or narrow surface. It involves carefully navigating difficult terrain, often requiring balance and precision, to move from one point to another without descending or ascending vertically. Traversing is common in slot canyons where the walls are steep or difficult to climb.

Up-Climb - a technique used to ascend (or overcome) an obstacle in the canyon. This is not too common in canyoneering as down-climbing is much more frequent, but sometimes in canyons, there are rock falls or oddly placed logjams that require you to climb up. Some canyons, such as "Sandthrax" has a certain 5.9 off-width rock climb! That obstacle takes serious effort! (See Module 29 - "Moving (Sequencing) in a Slot Canyon)

Webbing - refers to a type of strong, flat nylon or polyester material used for various applications, including creating anchors, slings, and harnesses. It is valued for its lightweight and durable properties, making it an essential component of canyoneering gear. Webbing can be sewn or tied into loops to form slings, which are used to attach to anchors or create harnesses. It is also commonly used in anchor systems and for constructing rappel setups. Webbing comes in different widths and strength ratings, typically measured in kilonewtons, ensuring that it can handle the loads experienced during rappelling and climbing.

Zion - the CORRECT name for Zion National Park. NOT Zions National Park. (Notice the difference?)

Zions - Typically this is said by ignorant Utahns who refer to Zion National Park as "Zions". They may say "hey, are you guys going down to "Zions" this weekend? While it makes my eyes twitch when I hear a Utahn (who SHOULD know better) say it that way...this is what they are referring to. (It would be similar to someone saying "Hey, are you going to San Diegos? or New York Cities? or Moabs? or Canadas? etc.) The confusion comes from a national bank headquartered in Utah called "Zions Bank". In the inner canyoneering circles, and while its extremely fun to make fun of sport culture, among my friends we will say to each other "Hey man, I'm going to down to Zionz National Bank Park this weekend - anyone else wanna come?" Or "I'm going to Moabs for some rappelling". We get a kick out of it. I mean kicks.

Canyoneering is a TEAM sport

Module 9

"In life, sometimes you learn that you are not a a very good team!"

Canyoneering emphasizes teamwork and group safety over individual talent. The goal is to ensure everyone exits the canyon safely, which requires understanding core skills like efficient rappelling.

Rappelling is often the biggest timewaster, but techniques like down-climbing or setting up the next rappel while another is rappelling can save *significant* time. For example, my group cut Imlay Canyon time from 17 to 8 hours by using efficient teamwork and reducing group size.

While efficiency is important, remember, canyoneering is not a race. Prioritize safety but, to be blunt, you need to always consider the group's slowest member.

Another point to make that can contribute to complicated problems VERY quickly – **STAY together as a group**! Even if some are fast or slow, generally stay within earshot of the entire group!

People usually split up from the group because they become emotional or stressed. This is a MAJOR problem. Work with the group to solve this issue. Communicate!

EVERY person is part of the TEAM and therefore has a vote/veto in the process. You (they) will see things that the leader doesn't see, hear things the leader doesn't hear, know things the leader doesn't know. The trip leader can easily make a mistake, so they should check the leader, the leader should check on them and we should all check each other throughout the day.

The IMPACT alone as functioning as a TEAM has a big impact on group safety. People have to speak up! Your literal life depends on it!

"You are only as fast as the slowest person."

WHY do you want to go Canyoneering?

Module 10

People are drawn to canyoneering for all kinds of reasons: the thrill of adventure, the challenge of exercise, or just tagging along with a friend doing "cool" things. For most, it is about discovering incredible places (and experiences) only a lucky few will ever see!

- Canyons need advocates to protect and preserve their beauty. Let us keep them accessible for everyone.

- Whether you are tackling an advanced canyon or loving the simplicity of the Subway, for example - your experience is YOURS. Do not let others diminish it (because unfortunately, it happens!)

- Variety is the spice of life! Descend "the best", "duds", "meh", and other under-rated canyons - the passed-up canyons often hold the memorable surprises.
- Do not be "that person" who claims to know it all. The canyon will quickly remind you otherwise (see Dunning-Kruger effect).

- Do NOT over-estimate your skills and under-estimate the canyon.

- Take it slow - master the basics, build confidence, and progress to harder canyons safely. Rome was not built in a day, and neither are great canyoneers.

- Don't fall for **FOMO** (Fear of Missing Out)! The canyons will always be there. Focus on soaking in the adventure - not conquering (through) it.

- **Remember** the Three golden rules of canyoneering:

    1. Be safe. (Seriously and always, safety first.)

    2. Have fun. (Because that is the whole point!)

    3. Always follow them in that order.

- Take your time, enjoy the adventure, and **record** (photos, videos, journal entry) the canyon and your **experience** for every canyon that you visit.
- Lastly, help others by **giving back to the canyoneering community**.

WHERE do you go Canyoneering?

Module 11

Wondering where to start? While most "big" canyons are known, countless smaller slots remain undiscovered or rarely descended due to tough access or effort required.

Canyons are typically found in deserts, especially where soft Navajo sandstone has eroded over thousands of years. Think of them as the "**sewer**" systems of the land.

Utah is the canyoneering mecca, with over **650** documented slot canyons on the **Colorado Plateau**. It is a hotspot for locals and global canyoneers alike! Many that live outside the US will do a yearly trip to the States to do a week or two of canyoneering.

For Utah residents/visitors, many slot canyons are just 4–5 hours from Salt Lake City, perfect for day or longer weekend trips.

To plan your adventure, you will need "***beta***"—route information about conditions, anchors, obstacles, and water levels.

Beta evolves with nature: flash floods, weather, and shifting sand can change a canyon's layout overnight. What was dry may now require swimming!

The Subway in Zion National Park is a prime example—it often changes drastically after storms.

Start by learning the Canyon Rating System (see **Module 17**). Then, explore beta resources online to find canyons suited to your skill level and group.

Here are some of the most popular beta resources on the web. Look at the region where you would like to go, then look at some of the names, followed by the canyon rating system. Then you will be able to decide which canyon is appropriate for you and your group.

Keep in mind, **not all beta is created equal**! In my canyoneering experience, www.climb-utah.com and canyoneeringUSA.com have the most consistent reliable beta content. RopeWiki.com is probably my 3rd choice (as it is user submitted, and there is no standard for consistency for submission. While other beta may be good on their website, others are going to be drastically different!

My advice - I would double or triple-check other beta sources for the same canyon.

CanyoneeringUSA.com

BluuGnome.com

Climb-Utah.com

RoadtripRyan.com

DyeClan.com

RopeWIKI.com (most active, currently)

Canyon Access & Land Types

Module 12

Canyoneering access depends on land type:

Federal: Includes BLM, Forest Service (FS), and National Park Service (NPS) lands.

State: Governed by individual states; access may vary.

Private: Owned by individuals/entities; permission is absolutely required.

Federal Lands:
- **BLM** (Bureau of Land Management): Open for canyoneering without permits or fees.
- **FS** (Forest Service): Access varies; research required.
- **NPS** (National Park System): Permits often required (e.g., Zion or Arches National Parks). Violations will lead to fines or court appearances.

State Parks: Access and regulations vary. For example, Goblin Valley State Park requires a permit and fee.

Private Land: Permission is mandatory. Trespassing harms the community and may permanently close access. Some incredible canyons exist on private land; respectful outreach is crucial.

Join the **Coalition of American Canyoneers** to support canyon access and preservation. Membership is currently free! Always follow regulations and promote responsible use to ensure access for future adventurers.

https://www.AmericanCanyoneers.org

Internet vs. Professional Instruction

Module 13

Canyoneering combines hiking, climbing, swimming, and rappelling through canyons. While reading about canyoneering can provide valuable theoretical knowledge, such as from this training, please opt in for professional training and hands-on experience before your first canyon.

Why Not Just Use Internet Instruction?
- Limited Perspective: Online guides and videos provide general advice but often lack context or specificity for real-world scenarios. I will do my best here to go beyond the mark and provide the best lecture-based training.
- Lack of Feedback: Internet resources cannot correct mistakes, provide tailored guidance, or adapt to your learning pace.
- Overconfidence Risk: Reading or watching videos can create a false sense of preparedness, leading to dangerous situations in the canyon.

Why Professional Canyoneering Training Matters:
- Safety First: Learn to assess and mitigate risks like flash floods and equipment failure. Gain life-saving emergency preparedness skills.
- Technical Skills Development: Hands-on training for rappelling, knot tying, route finding, and proper equipment use.
- Real-World Application: Adapt skills to unique canyon challenges and practice critical decision-making in real-time scenarios.
- Mentorship and Guidance: Expert instructors provide personalized feedback, while peer learning fosters collaboration and growth.

Additional Benefits of Professional Training:

- Confidence Building: Progress through foundational to advanced skills, gaining confidence for tackling more complex canyons.
- Legal & Ethical Knowledge: Learn local laws, permit requirements, and Leave No Trace principles for responsible participation.
- Community & Networking: Connect with like-minded enthusiasts for future adventures and access expert recommendations.
- Physical Conditioning: Understand the fitness demands of canyoneering and integrate mental and physical skills through practice.

If local training is not available:

- Join online forums to learn from other experienced canyoneers, at the very least. Get exposure to them and see what they notice, what they talk about or what systems or techniques they mention.
- Look for free workshops through the American Canyoneering Association (announced on their Facebook page).

There are a growing number of social media pages to follow and to supplementary learn from, (including introducing yourself and expressing a desire to meet-up in person) are:

- **Facebook**: "Canyoneering101"
- **Facebook**: "Art of RopeWork"
- **Facebook**: "Utah Canyoneers"
- **Facebook**: "Utah Canyoneering Explorers"
- **Facebook**: "Zion Canyoneering"
- **Facebook**: "Pacific Northwest Canyoning"
- **Facebook**: "SoCal Canyoneering"
- **Facebook**: "AZ Canyoneers"
- **Facebook**: "Canyon Rigging"
- **Facebook**: "Vancouver Canyoning"
- **Facebook**: "Canyon Gear: shop/swap, discuss, etc."

Please be objective in what you learn, and when in doubt, ask a more experienced canyoneer about it, or ask the online canyoneering communities before blindly following.

WHAT to expect in a Slot Canyon?

Module 14

...Depends on <u>Who</u>, <u>What</u>, <u>When</u>, <u>Where</u>, and <u>other</u> factors.

<u>Who</u> Are You Going With?
- **Friends or Family**: Expect slower progress and more assistance. Be prepared for a more cautious pace, especially with beginners.
- **Experienced Canyoneers**: Faster pace, self-sufficiency, and more adventurous decisions, like jumping or navigating risky obstacles.
- **Group dynamics** shape the canyon experience—expect different levels of engagement and comfort.

<u>What</u> Are You Doing?
- **Challenge, Aesthetics, and/or Fun**: Are you seeking a challenge or simply enjoying the experience? This determines how much effort and risk you are willing to take on.
- **Technical Focus**: If you are focused on learning technical skills, expect a more hands-on, slower-paced experience.

<u>When</u> Are You Going?
- **Spring**: Higher water levels due to snowmelt, which may require additional gear like wetsuits and create more challenging conditions.
- **Summer**: Drier conditions, fewer gear requirements, and easier canyon access—but beware of heat!
- **Fall/Winter**: Shorter days, colder water, and air temperatures. You will need extra layers, wetsuits, and headlamps. Expect more rugged conditions and fewer crowds.

Where you go canyoneering will matter:
- **Location Matters**: Canyons in different regions (e.g., Zion, Utah, Arizona) can have vastly different conditions. Some are wetter, some are drier, and some may require more technical skill or equipment. Research your destination for canyon-specific challenges and seasonal changes.
- **Accessibility**: Some canyons are more remote, requiring extra time or effort to reach. Others may be well-traveled, with more amenities and easier access but potentially more crowded.

Other Factors: Conditions Vary
- **Water Levels**: Can range from crystal clear to stagnant and smelly, depending on recent weather.
- **Obstacles**: One trip, you may swim through clear water; another, you might navigate over obstacles like dead animals or sand-filled potholes. Expect surprises!

Other Factors: Group Dynamics Influence Pace:
- The pace and difficulty of a canyon trip depend on the skill level of your group. Expect a more leisurely pace with beginners, and faster, more daring choices with experienced canyoneers.
- Everyone should be self-sufficient—if one person struggles, it affects the whole group's progress.

Other Factors: Planning Is Everything
- Always check the weather and plan for ideal conditions (blue skies). Going when rain is forecasted can turn your adventure into a dangerous survival situation.
- Know the canyon's specific conditions and prepare accordingly for the season.

Other Factors: Every Trip Is Unique
- Even repeat trips to the same canyon can be different. Water levels, weather, and your growing skill set make each adventure fresh and exciting.

- Reflect on the camaraderie and fun after the trip—it is not only about the canyon, but the memories you create with your group. The human experience is meant to be shared (in my opinion).

To whet your Canyoneering appetite, the following pages contain real photos of what to expect in *some* slot canyons. Remember, every slot canyon is different, and WHERE you go makes the difference.

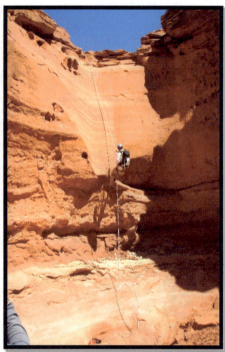

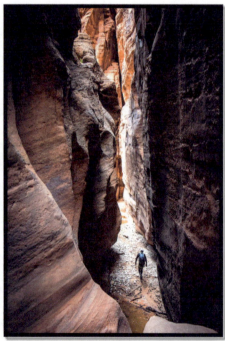

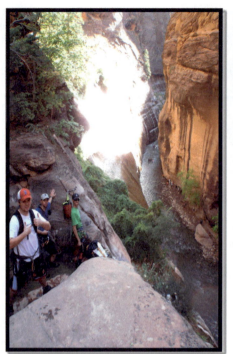

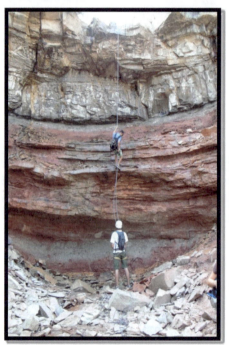
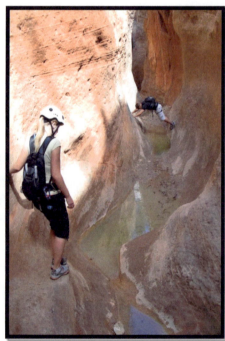

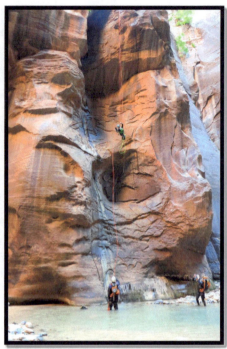

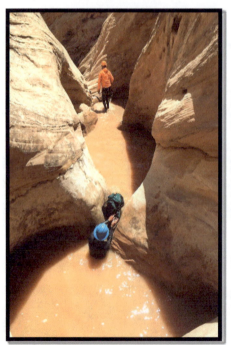

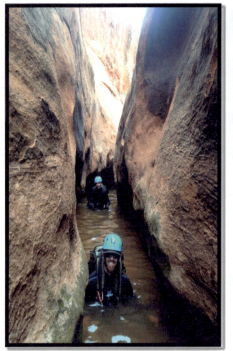

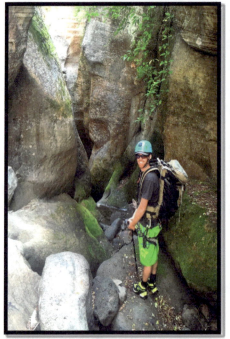

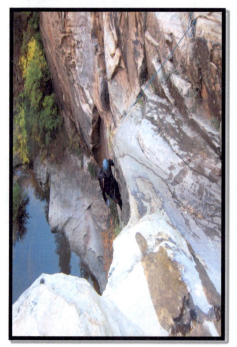

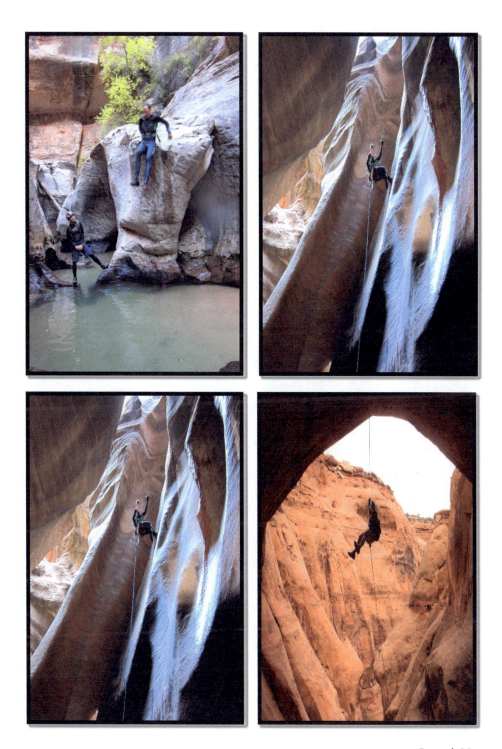

Slot Canyon Characteristics

Module 15

So, what are some of the characteristics of slot-canyons? Well, each single one has been carved and shaped due to a few factors: the rock type, the erosion and weathering process, geological structures, hydrology, and water features, and finally dimensions and scale of the slot canyon.

Rock Types:
- **Sandstone:** Smooth, undulating (smooth or wave-like) walls, vibrant reds, oranges, yellows.
- **Limestone:** Sharp edges, jagged walls, karst (i.e. caves) formations, dissolves in acidic water.
- **Granite:** Rugged, sharp-edged rock walls, challenging terrain, loose rock, steep drops.
- **Volcanic (Basalt):** Dark, rock columns, lava tubes.

Erosion & Weathering Processes:
- **Water Erosion:** Flash floods carve deep, narrow channels, creating dramatic canyon features.
- **Freeze-Thaw Weathering:** In colder climates, freeze-thaw cycles cause cracks in granite, leading to loosen debris.

Geological Features:
- **Stratification:** Distinct layers of rock due to sedimentary processes.
- **Unconformities:** Older rock sections exposed due to erosion, creating geological cross-sections (a profile view).

Hydrology & Water Features:
- **Waterfalls & Pools:** Seasonal features that vary, adding to navigation and aesthetic value.
- **Flash Flooding Risks**: Narrow canyons prone to trapping water, particularly dangerous in arid regions.

Dimensions and Scale:
- **Narrow Widths:** Ranges from a few inches to several dozen feet wide, creating dramatic shadows and lighting.
- **Verticality:** Steep, vertical walls can rise hundreds of feet, posing climbing challenges and offering stunning views.

Here are some *generalizations* of Canyoneering areas, depending on the time of year, just to give you an idea of *WHEN* to go:

Death Valley, California
- Spring: Popular, but rapidly warming
- Summer: Avoid—extreme heat (110-120°F)
- Fall: Still hot, shorter daylight
- Winter: Ideal, mild temperatures (60-70°F)

Cedar Mesa, Utah
- Spring: Popular, but cold water
- Summer: Popular, water-filled canyons, bugs
- Fall: Warm days, cold nights
- Winter: Short canyons, long exits, cold, snow possible

Escalante, Utah
- Spring: Moderate temps, snowmelt increases water
- Summer: High 90s, can be too hot
- Fall: Comfortable (70-80°F), shorter days
- Winter: Cold, snow on approach, short daylight

Lake Powell, Utah
- Spring: Popular, more water, wetsuits required
- Summer: Hot, water-filled canyons, bugs
- Fall: Least water, wetsuits needed
- Winter: Cold, wetsuits/drysuits, short days

San Rafael Swell, Utah
- Spring: Popular, water-filled canyons
- Summer: Hot, with more water
- Fall: Less water, wetsuits needed
- Winter: Cold, wetsuits/drysuits, short days

Moab & Arches N.P., Utah
- Spring: Great conditions, more water, some bugs
- Summer: Hot, but short canyons are doable
- Fall: Great conditions, warm days, cold nights
- Winter: Short canyons, cold, snow possible

North Wash, Utah

- <u>Spring</u>: Popular, little water
- <u>Summer</u>: Too hot for comfort
- <u>Fall</u>: Great conditions, little water
- <u>Winter</u>: Popular for "Freezefest," short daylight, snow possible

Zion National Park, Utah

- <u>Spring</u>: Popular, more water, wetsuits needed
- <u>Summer</u>: Popular, Hot, water-filled canyons
- <u>Fall</u>: Moderate temperatures, wetsuits needed
- <u>Winter</u>: Cold, snow possible, wetsuits/drysuits required

Module 16

Most canyoneering in the United States is found on a topographic feature called the Colorado Plateau. This area is primarily located in southern Utah, west Colorado, north-west New Mexico, and the northern part of Arizona.

The **Colorado Plateau** encompasses the four-corner states and region of the Southwest part of the United States. From the NPS.gov website, it says, "Originally named by John Wesley Powell, the Colorado Plateau comprises a series of tablelands (plateaus or mesas) located within an immense basin surrounded by highlands. Stream valleys that are typically narrow and widely spaced dissect the region, as do larger valleys, including the most spectacular – the Grand Canyon. "

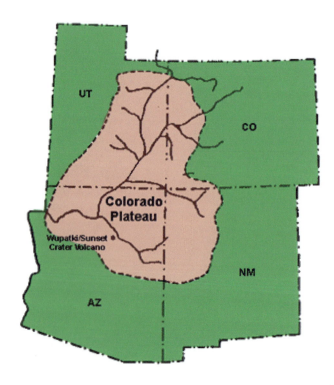

Colorado Plateau
- Found in southern Utah, western Colorado, northwestern New Mexico, and northern Arizona
- Contains one of the largest concentrations of slot canyons in the world
- Features: Plateaus, mesas, narrow stream valleys, and iconic landmarks like the Grand Canyon

Utah: Canyoneering Mecca
- Home to over 650 documented slot canyons, the highest concentration in the U.S.
- Considered the "mecca" for slot canyoneering

Other Notable Regions
- Arizona: Over 500 canyons, many slot canyons
- California: Over 700 canyons, but few true slot canyons (primarily found in Death Valley)

Canyons vs. "Routes"
- Canyons: Steep, narrow channels carved by water
- Routes: Larger drainage areas with rappels, downclimbs, and tricky navigation
- Both offer unique adventure opportunities, though routes may not involve true slot canyon experiences

Capitol Reef NP & area (Utah)

To start, the correct spelling is "capitol" and not "capital".

Location & Geology:
- Located in south-central Utah, part of the Waterpocket Fold, a unique geological feature (monocline) stretching nearly 100 miles
- Features layered geology, including Wingate and Navajo sandstone

Canyoneering:
- Over 30 documented canyoneering routes along the Waterpocket Fold
- Canyons primarily formed in sandstone, with rock types like shale, mudstone, gypsum, and limestone

Climate & Best Time to Visit:
- Arid climate, with average summer highs around 90°F
- Spring, summer, and fall are ideal; monsoon season (June-September) brings heavy rainfall and flash flood risks

Camping & Amenities:
- Fruita offers the best camping with showers, toilets, shade from cottonwood trees, and grassy areas
- Nearby Torrey has lodging and dining options

Popular Canyons:
- Pandora's Box
- Cassidy Arch Canyon
- The Wives
- Cottonwood
- Burro Wash

Beginner Canyons:
- The Wives
- Wife 5
- Wife 3
- Cassidy Canyon
- Stegosaur Slot
- Sunglow
- Cottonwood Wash (longer day)

Cedar Mesa area (Utah)

Location & Geology:
- Located south of North Wash, near the Hite Bridge area at Lake Powell
- Features bare rocks, high mesas, sheer cliffs, and deep canyons; Comb Ridge is a prominent topographic feature
- Geology includes light-colored sandstone in the west, transitioning to gypsum, shale, and limestone in the east

Canyoneering:
- Small concentration of technical slot canyons
- Canyons typically contain water, so wetsuits are recommended year-round; Flash floods are a risk, with past fatalities

Climate & Best Time to Visit:
- Best time to visit: Summer, as many canyons require water-based travel
- Flash floods can occur (some have been deadly), so always check weather forecasts

Camping and Amenities:
- Dispersed camping allowed on BLM land
- Hite Marina and Hanksville (1 hour away) offer services
- Bring all supplies (food, water, camping gear), as there are no nearby streams or creeks

Popular Canyons:
- Black Hole of White Canyon
- Rock Canyon
- Scar Tissue
- Fry Canyon
- Gravel Canyon
- Short Canyon
- Urban Cowboy
- Alcove Amble Canyon
- Horse Tanks
- Cowboy Canyon
- Cheesebox Canyon

Beginner Canyons:
- Short Canyon
- Ducket Slot
- Fry Canyon
- Black Hole
- Cheesebox
- Gravel

Escalante area (Utah)

Location & Geology:
- Located off the Hole-in-the-Rock Road, near Escalante, Utah
- Primarily contain Navajo sandstone, with dolostone, gypsum, and limestone

Canyoneering:
- Intermediate/Advanced canyoneers only: challenging canyons with long approaches and exits
- Keeper potholes and swimming required, especially after rainstorms
- Solitude likely, except for Neon Canyon (popular).
- Self-rescue is necessary; no cell service

Climate & Best Time to Visit:
- Best for Spring, Summer, and Fall; (Summer is hot and arid; but most canyons contain water)
- Consider seasonal rainfall and its impact on water levels in canyons (especially in Choprock Canyon)

Camping and Amenities:
- Dispersed camping is allowed on BLM land, but avoid camping at canyon entrances/exits
- Water sources: Springs, seeps, and the Escalante River (can be silty; use pre-filters or gravity filters)
- Nearest towns: Escalante and Boulder (about an hour from trailheads)

Popular Canyons:
- Neon Canyon
- Choprock Canyon
- Holy Cow
- Micro Death Hollow
- Davis
- Ringtail
- Egypt 1, 2, 3, 4
- Baker Canyon
- Headless Hen
- Coyote Gulch
- Zebra Canyon
- Peekaboo
- Micro Death Hollow

Beginner Canyons:
- Egypt 3
- Bull Valley Gorge
- Davis Gulch
- Death Hollow
- Egypt 1
- Dunham Slot
- Red Breaks
- Spencer Canyon
- Big Horn
- Zebra (Hiking/Scrambling)

Moab area, including Arches NP (Utah)

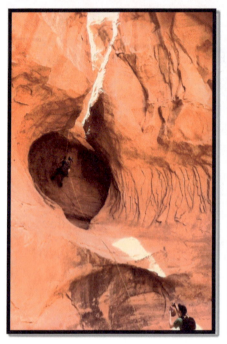 

Location & Geology:
- Located in South-Eastern Utah, near Arches and Canyonlands National Parks
- Known for sandstone formations; not primarily for slot canyons but offers many routes

Canyoneering:
- Over 28 documented canyons in the area, mostly easy and short; Few canyons may require swimming or wading
- Suitable for beginners, with many opportunities to practice rappelling skills
- Canyons are generally not technically difficult, but crowds can be an issue on weekends

Climate & Best Time to Visit:
- Summer: Peak season, but can be crowded
- Spring and Fall: Ideal for good weather and fewer crowds

Camping and Amenities:
- Moab offers plentiful lodging and food options
- The area is close to multiple outdoor recreation opportunities (hiking, rock climbing, mountain biking, 4-wheeling)

Popular Canyons:
- U-turn
- Tierdrop
- Dragonfly
- Granary
- Moonflower Canyon
- Entrajo Canyon
- Pleiades
- Rock of Ages
- MMI
- Winter Camp Slot
- Elephant Butte
- Repeat Jr
- Medieval Chamber
- Fins N Things
- Cameltoe
- Undercover
- Professor Creek
- Undercover Canyon

Beginner Canyons:
- Repeat Jr.
- Medieval Chamber
- Moonflower Canyon
- U-Turn
- Big Horn
- Tierdrop
- Winter Camp Slot
- Bow and Arrow
- Fins and Things
- Undercover
- Elephant Butte

North Wash area (Utah)

Location & Geology:
- Located north of Hite Marina, near Lake Powell
- Contains over 42 documented canyons, many of which are tight slot canyons

Canyoneering:
- Physically demanding canyons, even short routes can be exhausting
- Rappels are not particularly high but require problem-solving and strength
- Some canyons are especially challenging for larger individuals (Middle Leprechaun Canyon is particularly tough)
- Minimal water in the canyons year-round, though snow conditions can create unique winter challenges

Climate & Best Time to Visit:
- Spring and Fall: Popular seasons, though crowded (Winter: Cold, with potential snow conditions in the canyons)

Camping and Amenities:
- Main campground: Sandthrax Campground (often crowded, no on-site bathrooms or water); bring water (5-gallon containers)
- Hog Springs rest stop has a port-a-potty, about 10-minute drive from the canyon and Sandthrax Campground
- Nearest services: Hanksville (35-45 mins away) and Hite Marina (30-45 mins away)

Popular Canyons:
- Hogwarts
- Slideanide
- No Kidding
- Monkey Business
- Sandthrax
- Morocco
- Fooling Around
- Merry Piglet
- Irish Canyons (Shillelagh, Blarney, Leprechaun)
- The Hogs (1-4)
- Shenanigans
- Arscenic
- Woody Canyons

Beginner Canyons:
- Maidenwater, lower
- Lucky Charms
- Shillelagh
- Woodsy
- Hog 1
- Angel Slot
- Hogwarts
- Leprechaun
- Blarney

Robbers Roost area (Utah)

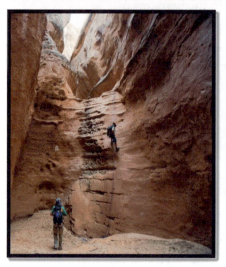 

Location & Geology:
- Located southeast of the San Rafael Swell, west of Canyonlands N.P., and north of North Wash
- Name originates from outlaws like Butch Cassidy using it as a hideout in the 1800s

Canyoneering:
- Features tight slot canyons similar to North Wash (Some canyons can be difficult for larger canyoneers)
- Minimal water in most canyons, though some may have puddles
- Protection for forearms and knees recommended due to abrasion from narrow canyons

Climate & Best Time to Visit:
- Best visited year-round, except summer (hot with little shade and little water)
- Avoid if rain is in the forecast, as roads can become impassable (Flash floods are concern during June to September)

Camping and Amenities:

- BLM land offers ample dispersed camping
- "Motel 6" campsite: Popular, often full-on weekends
- Nearest services: Hanksville (30-60 minutes away)

Popular Canyons:

- Bluejohn
- Alcatraz
- Larry
- Chambers
- Tidwell
- Moonshine Wash
- Mindbender Canyons
- Poison Spring Canyons
- Angel Canyons (Fallen Angel, Lost Angel, Angel Cove)
- Spur Canyons (Red, High, Low)
- White Roost

Beginner Canyons:

- Bluejohn, west
- Twin Corral Box
- Moonshine Wash
- Whist Roost
- Mindbender
- No Mans Canyon
- Maybe Mindbender
- Little Bull Canyon
- Low Spur

San Rafael Swell area (Utah)

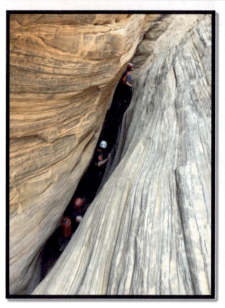 

Location & Geology:
- Located in southern-central Utah, part of the Colorado Plateau; Geologically unique as an anticline (fold)
- The San Rafael Reef surrounds the Swell, with jagged cliffs and deep canyons
- Common rock types: Navajo & Wingate sandstones, mudstone, and limestone

Canyoneering:
- Canyons feature potholes that can vary in depth after rainfall (may shift from shallow to fully submerged)
- Skill level: Ranges from beginner to intermediate, with challenges like keeper potholes and partner assists or bag tosses required for escapes
- Wetsuits recommended even on the hottest days

Climate & Best Time to Visit:
- Barren desert environment,
- Best visited in cooler months or summer heat (Wetsuits common, even in summer heat)

Camping and Amenities:
- BLM land provides dispersed camping options
- Water: Carry all supplies, as there are few natural springs; recommended to bring 5-gallon containers
- Nearest towns: Green River and Hanksville (30-90 minutes away), limited services and eateries

Popular Canyons:
- Knotted Rope
- Quandary
- The Squeeze
- Goblin's Lair (Chamber of the Basilisk)
- Eardley
- Buckeyes
- The Chute
- Black Box
- Little Wild Horse
- Ding and Dang
- Crack
- Chute
- Greasewood
- Zero Gravity
- Baptist Draw

Beginner Canyons:
- Little Wild Horse
- Ding and Dang
- Iron Wash
- Eardley
- Black Box, lower
- Goblin's Lair
- Zero G
- Greasewood

Zion NP and surrounding area (Utah)

Location & Overview:
- Refers to both Zion National Park and surrounding areas (including parts of St. George, over an hour away)
- Most frequented canyoneering destination in Utah with 55+ documented canyons

Canyoneering:
- Canyons range from beginner to expert levels, with 1-30 rappels and heights from 10 to 400 feet
- Rangers enforce permit compliance; violations result in citations, mandatory court appearances, and fines
- Wetsuits recommended for swimming canyons, especially in Spring, Summer, and Fall (except on the hottest days)
- Flash floods and rappelling accidents are a serious risk, particularly during monsoon season

Climate & Best Time to Visit:
- Best times: Spring, Summer, Fall (Beware during late summer: monsoon season - risk of flash floods)
- Wetsuits advisable for most canyons (check conditions in advance)

Camping & Amenities:
- Zion is surrounded by full-service towns (Springdale, St. George), with lodging, gas, food, and amenities available
- Crowds are common, especially during peak seasons—plan ahead!

Popular Canyons:
- Subway
- Keyhole
- Heaps
- Imlay
- Kolob
- Pine Creek
- Spry
- Mystery
- Echo
- Birch Hollow
- Behunin
- Englestead
- Orderville Gulch
- Fat Man's Misery (West)
- Johnson Arch Canyon
- Diana's Throne

Beginner Canyons:
- Keyhole
- Pinecreek
- The Subway
- Jolley Gulch
- Mighty Mouse
- Deadeye Dick Canyon
- Birch Hollow
- Mystery Canyon
- Echo Canyon (when full of water)
- Diana's Throne

Slot Canyon Ratings

Module 17

There is no official standard for canyoneering ratings, but the most used system is based on the **American Canyoneers Association** (ACA). Ratings describe the technical difficulty of a canyon, including:

- Technical Class (hiking to technical climbing/rappelling)

- Water levels (typical conditions)

- Time required (approach, canyon, and exit)

- Additional risks involved

Let me give you a few examples of **Canyon Ratings** and see if you can decipher it:

The Subway:	2B III
Bluejohn Canyon:	3A III
U-Turn Canyon:	3A I
Neon Canyon:	3B IV R

Let us discuss what these ratings signify!

Example: 2A III R

⬆ ⬆   ⬆   ⬆

In the first column: **Technical Class** (Range: Class 1, 2, 3, 4)

- Class 1: Non-Technical Canyon Hiking (no ropes required). Check route details for specifics. information.
- Class 2: Basic Canyoneering. Easy climbing/down-climbing; rope may help with handlines, backpacks, and assisting others. No fixed ropes needed for exits.
- Class 3: Intermediate Canyoneering. Rope required for rappels and technical climbing/down-climbing. Basic problem-solving needed to progress.
- Class 4: Expert Canyoneering. Includes all Class 3 obstacles and more. May contain multi-pitch rappels, advanced rope techniques, difficult potholes, extensive down-climbing, high stemming (20-60 feet), tricky anchors, long swimming sections, and numerous rappels (20+). Speed and efficiency are crucial.

The second column is: **Water Rating** (Range: A, B, & C.)

- Water Rating: "A": Normally dry, or may contain a little water after a rainstorm. Possibly, waist deep.
- Water Rating: "B": Normally a little current (or still, depending on conditions). Pools are to be expected, as well as swimming.
- Water Rating: "C": Normally a strong current flow. Waterfalls. Rope techniques for descending them are required (not taught on Canyoneering101.com).

The third column is: **Time Length/Duration** (Range: I, II, III, to VI). This combines the approach, canyon, and exit.

- Time Rating "I": Short. Requires 1 to 3 hours.
- Time Rating "II": Half-Day. Requires 3 to 6 hours.
- Time Rating "III": Half-Day to Full-Day. Requires 6 hours to at least 10 hours.
- Time Rating "IV": Full-Day. Requires more than 10 hours, but less than 24.
- Time Rating "V": Full-Day + 1.   Requires more than 1 day to complete.

The fourth (and optional) column: **Additional Risk** (Range: No Rating, R, X).

- (No Rating): If there is no rating listed here, then this canyon just has the assumed normal risks.
- Rated "R": At least one extraordinary risk may be present. Not for beginners (at all). Falling, drowning, risky anchors/rappels is possible. Solid technical skills MUST be in all individuals.
- Rated "X": More than one extraordinary risk is present. In addition to Rated R, Rated X canyons have the real possibility of seriously injuring and possibly death.

Unit 2: "The Essentials"

Modules 18 - 29

Welcome to Unit 2 - "**The Essentials**". This section covers the must-have skills and gear every canyoneer needs. Consider it the foundation for every canyon adventure.

While the "**Basics**" modules provide useful *context*, the "Essentials" are essential for canyon success!

If you are going on a one-time trip, you might not need everything on the list. However, if you plan to explore canyons long-term, these **gear items and knots** are a must.

Even if you are here for a **quick refresher**, it is a great idea! Revisiting the essentials ensures you are prepared for your canyon adventure!

Canyoneering Gear

Module 18

This module covers the must-have gear for most popular canyons on the **Colorado Plateau**.

While comprehensive, some canyons may require additional items or advanced canyoneering items (and skills).

- Essential Gear: Core gear needed for safe canyoneering, regardless of the canyon.
- Optional Gear: Specific to canyon conditions (e.g., water, potholes, rope length) and group needs.

Essential Gear (every canyon)

- Helmet
- Harness
- Descender/Rappel Device
- Rope(s)
- Canyoneering Shoes
- Backpack
- Personal Anchor System (PAS) | Safety Tether
- Carabiners (3 minimum)
- Quick Links (Rapides)
- Webbing
- Dry Bag
- Water Bottle/Reservoir/Bladder
- Headlamp
- Light Jacket/Rain Jacket/Extra Socks
- GPS
- First-Aid Kit
- LifeStraw (water-filter)
- Sunscreen

Optional Gear (canyon specific)

- Pull-Cord
- Rope Bag
- Full Wetsuit
- Shortie Wetsuit
- Drysuit
- Slings
- Booties & Socks
- Gloves
- Elbow Pad
- Knee Pad
- Radios
- Whistle

In technical slot canyons, rappelling and down-climbing in tight spaces pose risks from loose rocks falling from above. Rocks can be accidentally dislodged by others or from cliff ledges.

Wearing a **helmet** is crucial for protection—it is no longer just an optional accessory! Even experienced canyoneers cannot control what others do.

Helmets are required gear for all canyon adventures.
Most helmets are unisex, but some brands offer tailored versions for men or women.

My Suggestions:
- Petzl Elios
- Petzl Meteor
- Black Diamond Half Dome
- Black Diamond Vector
- Wild Country Synchro

Buy From:
- Petzl
- Black Diamond Equipment
- Mammut
- C.A.M.P. USA
- Grivel
- Wild Country

For long-term canyoneering, a comfortable **harness** with proper padding around the waist and leg loops is essential, especially on longer rappels.

The Black Diamond Momentum harness is a great choice—it is padded, comfortable for extended use, and includes two gear loops and a belay loop for secure connections.

Before purchasing, try on different models in-store (e.g., REI) to ensure a good fit. Harnesses come in both male and female sizes, with prices ranging from $40 to $150, offering options for different budgets.

My Suggestions:
- Black Diamond Momentum
- Petzel Corax
- Mammut Ophir
- Wild Country Syncro

Buy From:
- Petzl
- Black Diamond Equipment
- Edelrid
- C.A.M.P. USA
- Wild Country

A **descender device** connects you from your harness to the rope and controls your descent. For longer rappels, choose a device that allows friction adjustment and tie-offs mid-rappel. Devices like the ATC and Figure 8 work for shorter rappels (under 50 feet) but lack friction control for longer descents, especially if you weigh more than 140 pounds.

Popular options include the CRITTR, SQWUREL, and TOTEM. The SQWUREL (my favorite) allows friction adjustment but may twist the rope, so untwist before the next rappel. Always bring two descenders per person to avoid accidents like dropping one.

Before buying, ensure the device allows:
- Friction adjustment mid-rappel
- Tie-offs to stop during rappel

Once you have picked your device - find a safe, low-angled practice rappel spot and really get to know your descender! Try adding friction, tying off, experimenting with different speeds, and see if your device twists the rope.

My Suggestions:
- BluuGnome: SQWUREL v4
- CanyoneeringUSA: CRITR3
- Rock Exotica: Totem
- Black Diamond Equipment: ATC (as a backup too)

Buy From:
- BluuGnome.com
- CanyoneeringUSA.com
- Rock Exotica
- Black Diamond Equipment: ATC

Rappelling is a key part of canyoneering, requiring **ropes** designed specifically for the sport. Avoid hardware store ropes—they are not safe for climbing or rappelling. Instead, use static ropes from climbing companies.

Static vs. Dynamic Ropes:
- **Static ropes**: Limited stretch, lightweight, don't absorb water, and provide controlled rappels.
- **Dynamic ropes**: Designed for climbing, they stretch and absorb water, making them unsuitable for canyoneering.

Why Static Ropes Are Ideal:
- Minimal stretch for stable descents and heavy loads.
- Excellent knot security and durability on sharp, rough surfaces.

Beginner Recommendations:
- Start with 9 mm static ropes for better control and safety.
- **Suggested sizes** for beginners:
    - 120 ft for shorter rappels.
    - 210 ft for most trade canyons.
- Add a pull-cord (see Optional Gear: Pull-Cord) for rope retrieval.

As you gain experience, you can explore thinner ropes, but these require advanced friction management.

Pro Tip: Test your ropes and practice with them and your descender/rappel device before tackling real canyons!

Buy From:
- Imlay Canyon Gear
- BlueWater Ropes
- Sterling Ropes
- Atwood Gear

Canyoneering **shoes** are designed for durability, traction, and ankle support, making them essential for navigating slick sandstone and slippery potholes. Sneakers might work for short, simple trips, but serious canyoneers should invest in high-quality shoes.

Why they are special:
- Superior grip on slick surfaces.
- Ankle support for rough, wet, or rocky terrain.
- Pairs perfectly with neoprene socks for warmth.

Pro Tips:
- Size up 1/2 size to fit neoprene socks.
- Expect to spend $80–$300—your feet will thank you!

My Suggestion: La Sportiva: TX3/4 (as of 2025)

Buy From:
- La Sportiva: TX3, TX4
- Adidas: Canyoneer 3
- Salomon: XA Pro 3D
- Astral: TR1 Junction
- Merrell: Choprock Shandal
- Scarpa: Hydro Pro

At first glance, a canyoneering **backpack** may seem like a hiking pack, however, it is built for the unique challenges of canyons.

Features:
- Made from rugged materials (e.g., canvas or heavy-duty polyester) that resist rips from rocks and rough terrain—unlike standard hiking packs.
- Built-in grommets or mesh allow water to drain quickly, preventing the pack from becoming a soggy, 8-24 lb. anchor.
- Dedicated compartments for helmets, wetsuits, and gear make packing efficient and accessible.
- Fully waterproof packs keep gear dry but may sacrifice easy organization.

My Recommendations:
- Imlay Canyon Gear (brand),
- Slot (brand),
- Black Diamond (brand)
- Metolius: Free Rider (especially for Escalante area)

Pro Tip: For serious canyoneering, invest in a specialized pack. For occasional trips (e.g., The Subway in Zion), a hiking pack will suffice but expect wear and tear.

Buy From:
- Imlay Canyon Gear
- SLOT
- Osprey
- Black Diamond Equipment
- Metolius

Personal Anchor System (PAS) or Safety Tether

Module 18 – Essential Gear 7 of 18

A **Personal Anchor System (PAS)**, or "safety tether," is a must-have for canyoneering safety.

Purpose:
- Keeps you securely connected to the anchor while prepping your rappel ropes.

How It Works:
- A sturdy, closed-loop sling attaches to your harness (via girth hitch or carabiner).
- Provides a safe link to the anchor, especially on cliff edges with drops from 10–400 feet.

When ready to rappel, simply unclip your PAS from the anchor, reattach it to your harness, and descend safely on the rappelling rope!

My Recommendation:
- Sterling: Chain Reactor
- Petzl Connect Adjust

Buy From:
- Sterling: Chain Reactor
- Metolius: PAS
- Black Diamond Equipment: Link Lanyard
- Petzl: Connect Adjust

(3 minimum/person; screw-gate style)

Carabiner Essentials:
- Pronounced "care-a-bean-er"
- A rated **carabiner** is crucial for canyoneering safety.
- Look for kN markings (e.g., "kN 17"). One kN ≈ 225 lbs. of force.
- Bring at least 3 locking, screw-gate carabiners per person

Force and Falling:
- Force = Mass x Acceleration (measured in newtons or kN).
- Gravity accelerates you at 9.8 m/s² (32 ft/s²).

Why It Matters:
- A short fall (10 ft): Generates ~2.5 kN (560 lbs. of force).

- A longer fall (20 ft): Doubles speed, generating ~5 kN (1,120 lbs. of force).
- Anchors must absorb this force; weak anchors (e.g., bushes, roots, logs, bolted anchors) can fail.

Pro Tips:
- Avoid bouncing on rappel—it increases force on anchors and ropes!
- Carry multiple carabiners and always inspect your gear and anchor setup!

My Suggestion: No preference, as long it is a screw-gate carabiner for Southwest United States.

Buy From:
- Petzl
- Black Diamond Equipment
- Metolius

Purpose:
Quick Links (or Rapides) connect ropes to anchor points and are designed for the rappelling and knot points at the anchor.

Material:
Made of stainless steel or aluminum, they are durable and affordable, making them suitable for leaving behind when necessary.

How to Use:
1. Tie webbing to a natural or fixed anchor using a water knot.
2. Attach the quick link to the webbing.
3. Thread your rappelling rope through the quick link—NOT the webbing!

Never rappel on a rope directly through webbing. Friction can **easily** cut through webbing, just as ropes can cut through sandstone.

Buy From:
- Maillon Rapide (made by Peguet)
- Rock Exotica
- OnRopeCanyoneering.com
- REI.com
- RiggingWarehouse.com
- ElevatedClimbing.com

What Is It?

Flat, durable nylon or polyester strap used to create anchors and slings for securing rappelling ropes. Flexible enough to wrap around rocks, trees, or fixed anchors.

How Much to Bring:

Each person should carry at least **30 feet** to replace old or damaged anchors. Environmental wear and water can weaken webbing over time.

Safety Tip:
- Never trust webbing that "looks okay." Replacing it ensures reliability and safety.
- You will come across webbing in canyons. But is it one day old? One week or a year? Your literal life is dependent on the safety and webbing tying around that anchor - please be mindful.

Tying Webbing:
- Only use a water knot (see "Canyoneering Knots") and leave at least 3 inches of tail for security.

Buy From:
- REI.com
- Backcountry.com
- OnRopeCanyoneering.com

Why Use Dry Bags?
A garbage bag might seem like a quick fix to keep your pack dry in a wet canyon, but it's no match for technical canyons. One puncture, and your dry clothes (and lunch) will be ruined.

A Modern Solution:
Quality **dry bags** are widely available and reliable for keeping gear dry. Look for ones with built-in valves for added convenience.

Why a Valve Matters:
- Seal the bag by rolling down the top.
- Purge excess air through the valve for a compact fit.

- Ensures dryness while saving space in your pack.

Pro Tip:
- Don't forget to close the valve after purging!

Buy From:
- Sea to Summit
- Watershed
- SealLine
- NRS
- Aqua Quest
- Backcountry.com

Hydration is essential for safety in canyoneering. For the most part, you are in arid landscapes where there is typically, little water. Choosing between hard-cased water bottles (e.g., Nalgene) and water bladders/reservoirs depends on personal preference and the challenges of the canyon.

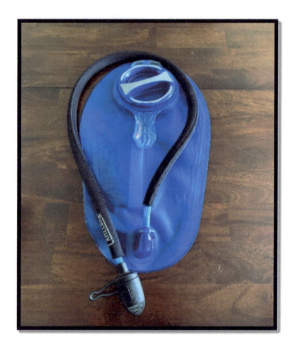

Water Bottles (e.g., Nalgene)
Pros:
- **Durability**: Can withstand rugged environments and accidental drops.
- **Ease of Cleaning**: Wide-mouth bottles are easy to clean and refill.
- **Versatility**: Doubles as a container for mixing drinks or storing items.

Cons:
- **Bulkiness**: Can be bulky in a pack and harder to access mid-hike.
- **Limited Capacity**: Usually holds less water compared to bladders.

Water Bladders/Reservoirs (e.g., CamelBak)
Pros:
- **Convenient Access**: Hose allows for hands-free drinking while moving.
- **Space-Saving**: Conforms to the shape of your pack for better weight distribution.
- **Larger Capacity**: Often holds 2-3 liters, reducing the need for frequent refills.

Cons:
- **Harder to Clean**: Narrow openings and long hoses can trap bacteria.
- **Puncture Risk**: Less durable than bottles in rough terrain.
- **Leak Concerns**: Damage can lead to significant or complete water loss.

My Recommendation:
- For short trips or technical/narrow/rugged canyons: Water Bottles for durability and simplicity.
- For long, endurance-heavy days: Water Bladders for convenience and capacity.

Pro Tip:
- Carry more water than you think you'll need! Don't forget to pack your LifeStraw and water purifier too.

Buy From:
- CamelBak
- Nalgene

Headlamp

Eventually, one of your canyon adventures will go long, and hiking out in the dark will be unavoidable.

Essential for Canyoneering

- Essential for exploring dark sections of canyons, tunnels, or sudden nightfall. Also, includes long canyon approaches before sunrise and long canyon exits after the sun has set.
- Keeps both hands available for hiking, sequencing, rappelling, or gear management.
- Illuminate's hazards like loose rocks, cliff drop-offs, potholes, or slippery surfaces.

Backup Essentials
- Extra Batteries: Ensure your headlamp remains functional throughout your trip.
- USB Power Bank with Cables: Recharge headlamps with built-in batteries or other essential devices like GPS units.

1. Choose the Right Headlamp:
- High lumens: 300+
- Adjustable beam settings (flood for general use, spot for detail).
- Water resistance/proof (IPX4 or higher).

2. Carry Spare Power Sources:
- Pack lightweight extra batteries (AA, AAA, lithium) or a compact power bank with appropriate cables too.
- Store batteries and cables in a waterproof container.

3. Test Before Leaving:
- Fully charge or replace batteries pre-trip.
- Check beam brightness and ensure the light and buttons works.

Buy From:
- Black Diamond Equipment
- Petzl
- Fenix Lighting
- REI

Why Layers Are Critical in Canyoneering

- Temperature Regulation: Slot canyons can be cold, especially after swimming or when the sun sets.
- Protection Against Elements: Rain jackets shield against sudden weather changes and hypothermia risks.
- Enhanced Insulation: Combining a lightweight jacket with a waterproof shell retains body heat well!

Waterproof Rain Jacket
- Waterproofing: Protects against rain
- Windproof Layer: Shields against wind chill in exposed areas, especially at rappel stations.
- Paired with Polartec AlphaDirect jacket, traps body heat while preventing rain/wind from entering.

PolarTec Alpha Direct (Warmest-to-weight ratio, jacket)
- Breathability: Allows moisture to escape, reducing sweat while keeping you warm. (My favorite part about it!)
- Lightweight and Packable: Easy to carry without adding bulk to your gear.
- Quick Drying: Ideal after swims in slot canyons or when it is cold on the approach and exit hikes.

Pro Tips for Layering in Slot Canyons
- Post-Swim Warmth: Wear jacket immediately after swimming to minimize heat loss.
- Add Rain Protection: Use a waterproof jacket over the lightweight layer for maximizing warmth.
- Store in Drybag: Keep jackets/socks/etc. stored in a drybag in case of water submersion.

Buy From:
- PolarTec
- DynaFit
- Skimo
- Darn Tough Vermont

GPS

A **GPS** with satellite capability is more than a navigation tool—it's a critical lifeline in the world of canyoneering! From communication updates to family members to sending out a SOS to local Search and Rescue (SAR) teams in times of emergency - they are worth the cost, especially as you cannot put a price on yourself, loved ones, friends, (and helpless strangers).

The Role of GPS in Canyoneering:

- **Emergency Communication**: Satellite-enabled GPS devices allow you to send SOS signals and communicate even without cellular service.
- **Trip Tracking**: Record your path for future reference or share with others for safety.

Key Features to Look For:

- **Satellite Messaging**: Ensures communication in areas with no cell service.
- **Topo Maps**: Topographic maps tailored for backcountry navigation. *
- **Weather Updates**: Receive critical forecasts to adjust plans (if your subscription plan offers it)
- **Durability**: Waterproof, shockproof, and designed for rugged use.

Pro Tips:

- Plan Ahead: Familiarize yourself with the GPS interface before heading out.
- Carry Backup Power: Bring a portable power bank to keep the device charged.
- Mark Key Points: Save waypoints for entry/exit, water sources, and hazards.

*NOTE - GPS/Satellite devices don't work well while IN slot canyons. But give it a try, however!

Buy From:

- Garmin GPSMap 66i (with satellite messaging plan)**
- Garmin inReach Mini 2 (with satellite messaging plan)**
- Garmin Montana 710i (with satellite messaging plan)**
- Garmin eTrex 22x (NO satellite messaging plan, but reliable, affordable GPS)**
- SavedBySpot: SpotX (with satellite messaging plan)**
- ZOLEO (with satellite messaging plan)**
- Starlink Direct-To-Cell (coming 2025 to T-Mobile)

** or newest model that they offer. But compare prices and features before purchasing to see what is appropriate for you!

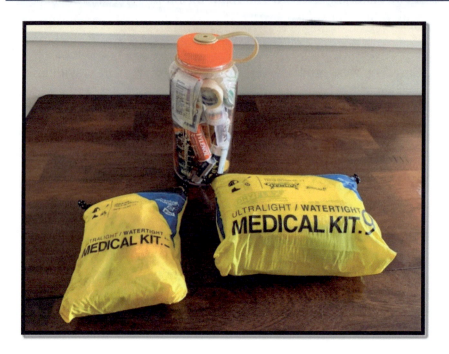

Why Bring a Kit?

In remote canyons, help may be hours or days away. A **first-aid kit** helps manage minor injuries, stop bleeding, and stabilize serious conditions (like a sprain or fracture) until help arrives.

Must-Have Supplies:

- Adhesive bandages, gauze, medical tape, antiseptic wipes
- Blister treatments (e.g., Moleskin), tweezers
- Personal medications and a pocket-size wilderness medical guide
- Keep it lightweight and waterproof (store in a drybag or case).

Emergency Preparedness:

- Stay calm, assess injuries, and decide if the team can continue or needs a rescue.

- Carry a satellite communicator or emergency beacon—cell service is rare.
- Ensure everyone knows basic first aid and canyon safety protocols before heading out.

A Personal Note:

As a Type 1 Diabetic, I carry insulin, syringes, and extra sugar in case of a low blood sugar—critical for my survival in remote areas and canyons where supplies aren't accessible for hours or days until you reach civilization again!

Buy From:

- Adventure Medical Kits

Lifestraw®

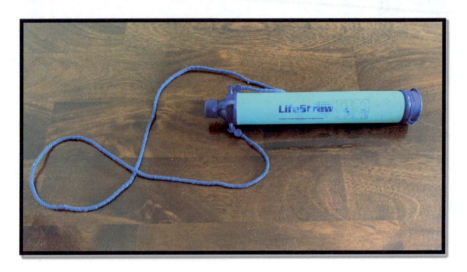

What is it?

A 2-ounce, pocket-sized **water purifier** that filters up to 1,000 gallons, removing bacteria, parasites, and microplastics. It lasts up to 5 years, has no expiration, and is easy to clean and store.

Why Carry One?

- **Lightweight**: Easy to pack and forget until needed.
- **Lifesaving**: A backup if you run low on water during desert adventures.
- **Affordable**: At ~$20 USD, everyone in your group can carry one.
- **Practical**: Use it to drink directly from streams, saving bottled water for dry stretches.

My Personal Thoughts:

While not essential for canyoneering, it is a reliable water backup. Keep one handy—you will be glad you did! I use mine all the time in canyons especially where I know where water is very limited, that way I drink the natural water first and save my portable water if there is a LONG hike out. Not always do I do that, but I do when in Escalante (except the Escalante River as it is very silty and plugs up filters).

Buy the original and alternatives from:

- LifeStraw: Personal Water Filter (original)
- Katadyn: BeFree Filter
- HydroBlu: SideKick
- Survival Filter
- Sawyer: Squeeze
- Sawyer: Mini

Sunscreen

Why You Need It:

- Protects your skin from sunburn and reduces skin cancer risk, especially in the sunny, exposed canyons of the American Southwest.

What to Pack:

- Sunscreen with SPF 30+ (recommended by the American Academy of Dermatology).
- A hat or buff as an alternative or extra protection.

<u>Pro Tip</u>:
- Reapply throughout the day, especially during long, sunny exit hikes!

What It Is:

A lightweight, static rope (usually 6 mm) that is used to retrieve your rappel rope when your rope is too short to double up.

Why Use It?

- Saves weight and space compared to carrying a full-length rope.
- Ideal for canyons with tall rappels (e.g., a 115-ft rappel needs only a 115-ft rope and a pull cord, not a 300-ft rope).
- Perfect for experienced canyoneers managing weight and gear.

Alternatives for Beginners:

- Bring an additional full-size rope to serve as both a backup and a pull cord.
- Follow the 3x Rule: For a 100-ft rappel, pack 3x 100-ft ropes—one for rappelling, one as a pull cord, and one as a backup. Or 1x 200-ft rope, and 1x 100-ft rope.

Pro Tip: Always plan for rope retrieval and backup in case of damage or loss!

Buy From:

- Imlay Canyon Gear
- BlueWater Ropes
- Sterling Rope
- On Rope Canyoneering

Why Use It?

- Keeps ropes organized, tangle-free, and ready to rappel.
- Prevents ropes from snagging, unraveling, or being lost on approach or exit hikes.
- Easy to secure - clip it to an anchor point to keep ropes safe until use.

Pro Tips for Use:

- For Pull-Cords: Keep the rope bag in place until the last person rappels to avoid twists and ensure clear identification of the rappel strand. Prevent accidents caused by rappelling on the wrong side of the rope!
- Listen for the "thud" as the bag hits the ground—this confirms your rope is long enough for the rappel in 99% of cases (still visually check if you are able).

Planning Reminder:

Always verify your rope's length against the canyon's longest rappel. A rope that is too short can have life-threatening consequences! Research your canyon thoroughly, choose your team and pack wisely!

Buy From:

- Imlay Canyon Gear
- BlueWater Ropes
- Sterling Rope

Why You Should Think About Getting One:

Canyons often contain cold, stagnant water trapped in shaded areas, staying chilly year-round. **Wetsuits** trap a thin layer of water against your skin, warmed by your body heat for insulation.

What to Look For:
Fit: Snug is better—loose wetsuits let in cold water.
- **Styles**: Full (previous photo), Shortie (next photo), or Farmer-John (not pictured)
- **Thickness**: Ranges from 1 mm (light) to 7 mm (warmest). Most canyoneers prefer 3 mm full wetsuits; women often choose 5 mm for extra warmth.
- **Labeling**: For example, a "3/2" wetsuit means 3 mm thickness for the core and 2 mm for arms and legs—warmer where you need it, flexible where you move.

A full wetsuit is ideal for canyoneering because it provides full-body protection against cold water, ensuring warmth in chilly, stagnant pools often found in deep, shaded canyons. It also offers abrasion resistance, protecting the skin from sharp rocks, sand, and rough terrain while navigating through the canyon. The coverage ensures that the entire body stays warm and protected, making it a must for long, cold water sections (but it depends on the canyon, and canyon conditions).

Buy From:
- O'Neill
- Rip Curl
- HyperFlex
- Xcel
- Big5 Sporting Goods

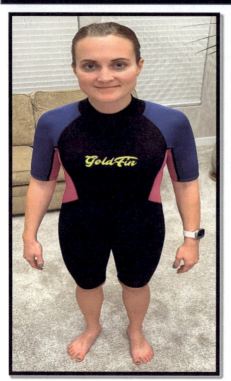

Do You Need One?

- A **shortie wetsuit** is a great choice when canyoneering in warmer water environments. It provides adequate protection for the torso and upper legs, ensuring comfort and flexibility while allowing better movement for climbing, scrambling, and active rappelling.
- Ideal for moderate temperatures, it offers some insulation without the bulk of a full wetsuit. Shorties are also more breathable, which can be beneficial for physical activities in warmer canyons.

What to Look For:

- Material: Neoprene is the most common material, offering both warmth and flexibility. Look for a thickness between 2-3 mm for moderate protection.
- Fit: Ensure the wetsuit fits snugly around the body, especially the torso, to maximize warmth retention and prevent water from flushing through.
- Seams: Sealed or glued seams provide better water resistance, which is important for keeping warmth in.

Shortie wetsuits are perfect for moderate temperatures and active movement (whereas full wetsuits are better suited for colder, more challenging canyons where greater warmth and full-body protection are required).

Buy From:

- O'Neill
- Rip Curl
- HyperFlex
- Xcel
- Big5 Sporting Goods

Unlike a wetsuit, a **drysuit** keeps you fully dry (except for your head, hands, and sometimes feet if it lacks built-in booties). Drysuits use gaskets—rubber seals around the neck, wrists, and ankles—to prevent water from entering. Even in below-freezing water, wearing just a t-shirt and sweatpants underneath can keep you comfortable. You will still "feel" the cold, but once out of the water, you warm up quickly.

Why Choose a Drysuit?

Drysuits are ideal for cold conditions or for canyoneers who have a low tolerance for cold but still want to experience canyoneering. They are perfect for icy canyons or long, cold swims. However, they come with a significant price tag, ranging from $800 to $2000. My favorite is the Level Six Emperor model, which is rugged, comfortable, and packs down small like a wetsuit, priced at around $1200.

Pros:
- Total Dryness: Keeps you completely dry (except your head and hands), even in cold, icy conditions.
- Comfort in Extreme Cold: Excellent for canyoneers who need protection from freezing water.
- Fast Drying After Use: You warm up quickly after exiting the water.
- Durable, sort of: High-quality drysuits are built to withstand tough environments, however, one puncture can let ice-cold water!

Cons:
- Cost: Drysuits are expensive, with prices ranging from $800 to $2000.
- Bulky: Although they pack down smaller than wetsuits, drysuits are still bulkier than basic gear.
- Comfort: Gaskets around the neck, wrists, and ankles can sometimes feel tight or uncomfortable, especially in older models.

Buy From:
- Level Six
- Kokatat
- Waterproof Diving

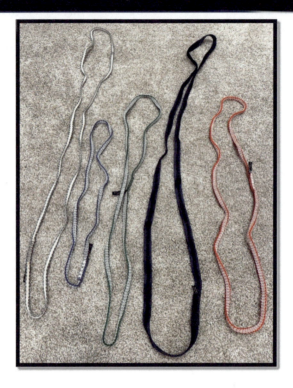

A **sling** (similar to a PAS) is an essential piece of canyoneering gear that connects your harness to anchors, attaches to gear like ascenders and tiblocs, and can be a lifesaver in unexpected situations—like lowering a backpack or adding extra length to a pull-cord.

Budget-friendly at $10-$30 each, having four or more slings on hand from the start is a good beginner recommendation.

As you progress in your canyoneering skills, slings become more critical, especially in advanced canyons or challenging features like potholes. They are versatile, compact, and reliable making them a must-have for any canyoneer.

Buy From:
- Imlay Canyon Gear
- Edelrid
- Black Diamond Equipment
- Petzl
- Metolius

Neoprene socks (also called "**booties**") are crucial for keeping your feet warm in cold, wet slot canyons. When wading through icy waters for hours with no sunlight, these booties are a lifesaver. While wearing wetsuits and booties in the summer desert may seem odd, it is all about functionality—not fashion.

For most canyoneers, 3 mm thickness provides optimal warmth, while 2 mm is suitable for milder conditions. Keep in mind that thicker booties may require larger shoes.

If no water is expected, I prefer merino wool socks, which provide cushioning and warmth even when wet. Consider packing an extra pair of hiking socks for the approach and exit hike—nothing beats the comfort of a dry pair for the hike out.

For product recommendations, check with canyoneering communities online for the best brands and tips.

While **gloves** are not required for canyoneering, they quickly become a game-changer after a few trips.

Canyoneering is tough on your hands, which are constantly used for climbing, gripping the rappel rope, and navigating rugged terrain. At the very least, gloves can help keep your hands warmer in cold conditions.

I usually bring two types of gloves:

- **Lightweight, rubber-dipped gloves** for general protection. These are great for climbing, clearing branches, and protecting my fingers in tight spaces.
- **Thicker rappelling gloves** for longer rappels (over 120 feet), helping to protect against rope heat caused by friction.

However, be cautious: gloves can mask poor rappel technique! If you are rappelling too fast, gloves might absorb some of the heat, but that is a BIG sign you need to improve your friction control rather than mask poor skill.

Mastering friction and managing rappel speed is crucial to prevent accidents (and falling great heights), including rope burns from an over-heated carabiner.

<u>Pro Tip</u>:
As you begin, always practice rappelling without gloves to understand how friction works with your descender device. Once you are comfortable with control, gloves will make your canyoneering experience a little more comfortable while protecting your hands (again, be careful on rappels with them!)

Elbow Pad

Elbow pads serve the same purpose as knee pads, but instead of protecting your knees, they safeguard your elbows and forearms. They are especially useful when navigating rough terrain, crawling through tight spaces, or rappelling in canyons.

Elbow and knee pads work together functionally, providing full-body protection during your canyoneering adventures. Having both ensures you stay comfortable and protected from scrapes, impacts, and fatigue during long treks.

Buy From:
- Anywhere that sells elbow pads, such as Walmart.com, Amazon.com or a bike shop.

Knee pads are essential for navigating narrow slots, climbing over boulders, or scraping along rough canyon walls. They protect against sharp rocks, abrasion, and the sandy grit that adds extra wear to your knees.

Knee protection helps prevent painful cuts, bruises, and fatigue during long canyoneering routes. They are lightweight, easy to pack, and provide crucial comfort when you need it most. A small investment for significant protection, ensuring you can push through tough terrain without discomfort.

Buy From:
- Anywhere that sells elbow pads, such as Walmart.com, Amazon.com or a bike shop.

While you likely will not need a **radio** during most of your canyon trip, there are key situations where it becomes invaluable. On long approach hikes, where your group may be spread out, or in areas with noisy waterfalls and rappels, radio communication helps keep everyone connected.

Water-resistant or waterproof radios are especially useful for coordinating rappels, ensuring safety, and resolving issues quickly— such as confirming if someone has made it down safely or alerting others to falling rocks.

While not "essential," a radio becomes crucial for rappels over 100 feet, navigating noisy waterfalls, or handling long approaches and exits. It is a small investment for significant peace of mind.

Buy From:
- Rockie Talkie
- Midland
- Cobra
- Retevis
- Uniden

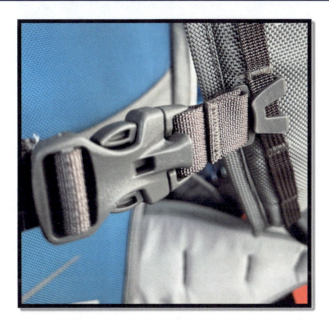

A **whistle** should serve as either a primary communication tool or a reliable backup to your radio. It's a cheap, waterproof alternative that works in situations where radios might not be effective.

Many backpacks, like the 'Slot,' even come with a built-in whistle for convenience!

Just like radios, whistles are especially important for rappels over 100 feet, in canyons with waterfalls, or during long approach and exit hikes. However, unlike radios, you will need a pre-established signaling system. One short blast could mean "all clear" or "I'm down," while multiple long blasts indicate "emergency."

Be sure everyone in your group knows and practices the communication system.

Protection is about more than just gear—it is about anticipating the conditions and equipping yourself accordingly. Whether you need to guard against abrasions from sand, stay warm in cold water, or shield yourself from the intense desert sun, it is important to pack with purpose. Essentials like helmets, wetsuits, drysuits, knee and elbow pads, gloves, and sunscreen are all part of the equation. Many of these items overlap with general "gear," but viewing them through the lens of protection ensures you are thinking about the environment and its challenges with YOUR survival.

When you approach each canyon with a mindset or framework that **balances the items you are bringing and the protection they provide, you are less likely to forget critical gear**—whether it is a spur-of-the-moment trip with 10 minutes to pack or a major expedition planned over weeks. Framing your preparation this way not only minimizes accidents but also equips you to handle those inevitable "what if" or "uh-oh" moments with more confidence.

The following items qualifies as canyoneering protection:

- <u>Head Protection</u>: Helmet
- <u>Body Protection</u>: Full Wetsuit/Shortie/Drysuit
- <u>Knee Protection</u>
- <u>Elbow Protection</u>
- <u>Hand Protection</u>
- <u>UV Protection</u>

<u>Head Protection</u>: **Helmet** - Canyons are rugged, with potential of falling rocks (especially when rappelling), so always protect your head in every technical canyon.

Body Protection: **Wetsuit** - Essential for cold water; even in the summer, canyon water can be very chilly! In alpine canyon settings, a dry suit might be a better option to stay warm. A wetsuit works by trapping a thin layer of water between your skin and the neoprene. This thin layer of water warms up due to conduction from your body's heat. **The recommendation is 3 mm to 5 mm**. Anything lower does not add much thermal protection, but it would be better than nothing. You can invest in a high quality one with less seams or that has seam protection. Less seams or one with seam protection makes it more comfortable when it is pressed against your body all day long (my wife suggested that point that I overlooked!).

Body Protection: **Drysuit** - a must have for winter canyoneering when water temps are frigid, helping you stay dry and insulated. Drysuits differ from wetsuits as they have gaskets around your neck and arms typically and you must squeeze your body into it. I've done a few frigid canyons wearing only sweatpants, a t-shirt, and fleece on top and have been adequately okay. Not cold but not hot but have just enough maneuverability in them. Invest the time into research and save some money (most are $1000+) if you are serious about winter canyoneering.

Knee protection: Perfect for narrow, "skinny" canyons where you might be high-stemming or scraping your knees on rough rock. Always good to keep these in your pack, just in case.

Elbow protection: Like knee protection, **elbow guards** are great for those tight, narrow spots where you elbows take a beating too. These are also easy to store and pull out as needed.

Hand protection: in other words, **gloves**. Durable, rubber-dipped gloves under $10 work best to guard against scrapes will still offering decent grip on cold rock.

UV Protection: **Sunscreen** is vital for desert trips! Or at least a hat or buff. A SPF above 30+ is recommended for your neck, face, and arms from painful sunburn and to reduce the risk of skin cancer. **Sunglasses** are another MUST HAVE for the desert sun.

Canyoneering Gear Loadouts

Module 20

What does a gear load-out look like with all your gear for your first, technical slot canyon?

On this page, I will cover just that so you can get an idea of what a canyon trip *could* look like.

As always, as it is in canyoneering - "**it depends**." It depends on what canyons you are descending, **who** you are bringing (beginners vs. experienced vs. young vs. older), and **when** you are going (Winter, Spring, Summer, Fall) and more.

Short Day, Dry Canyon

- Backpack
- Helmet (not pictured)
- Harness
- Canyoneering Shoes
- PAS
- Carabiners
- Descender Device:
    - SQWUREL
    - TOTEM
    - ATC (backup)
- Quick Links (Rapides)
- 30 ft of black Webbing
- Gloves
- 200 ft rope
- 200 ft pull-cord
- First-Aid Kit
- GPS (w/Satellite Messenger)
- Headlamp
- Radio
- LifeStraw

Full Day, Dry Canyon

- Backpack
- Helmet (not pictured)
- Harness
- Canyoneering Shoes
- PAS
- Carabiners
- Descender Device:
  - SQWUREL
  - TOTEM
  - ATC
- Quick Links (Rapides)
- 30 ft of black Webbing
- Gloves
- 200 ft rope (9 mm)
- 200 ft rope (9 mm) *someone else carries
- 120 ft rope (9 mm) *someone else carries
- 200 ft pull-cord
- First-Aid Kit
- GPS (w/ Satellite Messenger)
- Headlamp
- 2-way radio
- LifeStraw

Full Day, Wet & Dry Canyon

- Full Wetsuit (4/3 mm)
- Bigger Backpack
- Helmet (not pictured)
- Harness
- Canyoneering Shoes
- PAS & Slings
- Carabiners
- Descender Device:
    - SQWUREL
    - TOTEM
    - ATC
- Quick Links (Rapides)
- 30 ft of black Webbing
- Gloves (Rubber and Rappelling)
- 200 ft rope (9 mm)
- 200 ft rope (9 mm) *someone else carries
- 120 ft rope (9 mm) *someone else carries
- 200 ft pull-cord
- First-Aid Kit
- GPS (w/ Satellite Messenger)
- Headlamp
- 2-way radio
- LifeStraw

Full Day, Wet & Dry Canyon - Extra Cold!

- Drysuit
- Biggest Backpack
- Helmet (not pictured)
- Harness
- Canyoneering Shoes
- PAS & Slings
- Carabiners (with extras)
- Descender Device:
    - SQWUREL
    - TOTEM
    - ATC
- Quick Links (Rapides)
- 30 ft of black Webbing
- Gloves (Rubber and Rappelling)
- 200 ft rope (9 mm)
- 200 ft rope (9 mm) *someone else carries
- 120 ft rope (9 mm) *someone else carries
- 200 ft pull-cord
- First-Aid Kit
- GPS (w/ Satellite Messenger)
- Headlamp, waterproof
- 2-way radio
- LifeStraw & Water filter
- Alpha-Direct Mid-layer
- Waterproof/Windproof Jacket Shell
- Pothole Escape Tools
- Handled Ascenders (or similar)

Canyoneering Knots Overview

Module 21

At Canyoneering101.com (and including this book) I have selected a set of "essential" knots that provide the foundation or building blocks to knot-tying. Because what you tie does matter! **In fact, it is life or death based on if you tie these correctly or not!** Look at this list in a **linear way** where you progress forward. It all starts with the knowing what webbing is, of course, but starting formally with the Overhand knot.

Mastering (and/or memorizing) these knots will give you a strong technical foundation for your canyoneering career - because that is the whole point of this website! **Sure, there are hundreds of knots out there, but learning 40 of them will not do you much good if you cannot confidently tie 10 of them when you need them most**.

Essential Canyoneering Knots:

Webbing (what is it?)
Overhand
Water Knot
Figure 8 Knot
Figure 8 Knot - On a Bight
Figure 8 Knot - Follow-Through
Clove Hitch/Triple-Clove Hitch
Munter Hitch
Girth Hitch
Stone Hitch
Figure 8 Bend
EDK Bend
Double-Fisherman Bend

You will find these in the chapter: **"Canyoneering Knots"**. Each of them will have their own dedicated page.

They contain step-by-step pictures on how to tie them, including their purpose, their pros and cons, and scenarios where you would use that specific knot.

Canyoneering Anchors

Module 22

Anchors in canyoneering are what we attach ourselves to while descending a canyon so that we can safely rappel or down-climb with rope assistance. Not all anchors are created equally!

There are 4 different types of anchors:

- Natural,
- Fixed (or "man-made"),
- Retrievable, and
- "meat" anchors.

Natural Anchors:

These consist of "**natural**" things found in the environment. Rocks, boulders, tree trunks, roots, etc. These are the preferred anchor of choice as we as a community is not bringing in gear which will permanent in the walls. These anchors have mostly stood the test of time. However, do not assume that just because it is attached to a tree, that it is safe! Every anchor needs to be examined before using it.

- **Dead Man Anchors**: wrapping webbing around a carryable-size rock that you bury in the sand and rappel from that.
- **Cairn Anchor**: wrapping webbing around a carryable-size rock that you stack on top of the ground, which is then fortified by other large boulders/rocks to hold that initial rock in place. Once verified for weight, you rappel from that.

Fixed Anchors (or known as "man-made"):

These anchors are the "**permanent**" type which are literally drilled into the rock. There are different types of these as they can consist of bolts, hangars and pitons. Beginners erroneously put their trust in these over natural anchors at first because there is some notion that it is "safer".

Some **bolts** and **hangers** have been securely fastened or glued into a work and has stood for decades. Other bolts have been drilled incorrectly, installed incorrectly, placed incorrectly, and not glued-in correctly. There have been some stories of where bolts have failed (typically because they fall into the aforementioned reasons)!

Ultimately - Do not assume that just because it is attached to the rock, that is safe!

Every anchor needs to be examined before using it!

Retrievable Anchors:
This type of anchor is deployed around a technique called "**Ghosting**". That means to leave no evidence of your descent, including webbing and anchors. There are ways to tie anchors around natural and fixed anchors so that you can retrieve your anchor after everyone is done rappelling. One must need to be proficient with technical rope work before deploying this, otherwise you could get a rope stuck (and someone needs to climb UP the rope to get it unstuck) which may have disastrous results for your party! **This is NOT taught in-depth in this book or Canyoneering101.com.**

Meat-Anchors:
A meat anchor refers to when we use our literally physical **body** as a counterweight to the rappeler or down-climber. We do this when no natural or fixed anchors are to be found or used! Extreme caution must be used as bodily injury or death may result if not properly used or deployed. Generally, there should be more than one-person on a "meat" anchor when a person is rappelling. The last person down will not have the assistance of a "meat" anchor and so the people at the bottom must have a way of "capturing" them. **This is NOT taught in this book or on Canyoneering101.com**

Module 23

This page will focus on how to examine your natural or fixed anchor.

As per our usual theme - you MUST examine EVERY anchor. Do not assume that anything you rappel on or see will be safe. Generally, people will be okay if caution and skill are exercised.

When you get to anchor, you must always inspect it.

If you first notice many strands of webbing, it's practice to remove it all and tie a new piece of webbing in its place. Many times, assume that more strands equal better! Not true! In fact, it could be dangerous as the next suspecting party may assume to use it and think all is well, when it's actually not!

When you look at the webbing, you are looking for cuts, frayed ends, sun-fading, burn marks, or stiffness. This all signifies that the webbing is old and needs replacing. Again, this is why everyone in you party needs at least 30 feet of webbing at a minimum. Sometimes double and triple that amount in canyons with many rappels.

Once the webbing check is completed, look at the knot. Is the water knot tied correctly? Is there at least 3" of tail on both ends? Is it tied around the natural or fixed anchor correctly? If not, replace it. Do you have a "hunch" or any worry about it? Then, replace it.

There is a correct way to making sure that your anchor is equally loaded. What this means is that if one anchor (or bolt) or natural anchor fails, then your redundant or backup anchor will hold you in place. But you cannot just stretch your webbing from anything that you see. In fact, doing that may put MORE force on your anchor and have more of a chance of failing!

Look at the anchor point and make sure that you are equalizing off of a 60-degree angle or below! This means between the webbing and the two anchor points on the wall or natural anchor. Anything higher than 60 degrees puts more than half the load on each anchor point, sometimes even doubling and tripling the force weight.

Rope 101

Module 24

All you need to know about ropes for canyoneering. This will cover rope terminology, the different types of ropes used in the sport, and how to protect or prolong its life.

There is a "rule" out in the canyoneering community that says you need to bring 3x the amount of rope of the tallest rappel. This isn't a "rule" per-se, but more of a really good guideline. There have been many canyons where I have not brought 3x the amount of rope. It's just a lot of weight!

However, bringing at least 2x the amount is considered a best practice. Let me provide an example - if your tallest canyon is 80 feet, then bringing 160 feet should get you okay. It isn't sufficient enough to bring just 1x 100-foot rope, and assume everything will be okay... What if it got snagged when you were trying to retrieve it? What if you dropped the rope bag on your way to the anchor? What if...? What if…? Suppose, you didn't have an extra rope - you and your group would be literally stuck for who knows how long?! That's not a great predicament to be in! But if you brought another 100-foot rope, then you could easily rig that one up, rappel down to where the other rope is stuck, get it free, and continue on. In fact, you wouldn't even lose much time over it.

I would suggest bringing two ropes in which lengths are over the tallest rappel length, plus a small 6mm as your pullcord and/or your emergency rope. It is not much extra weight. And this is just the cost of canyoneering to help assure you have redundancy and bring more peace of mind in case things go wrong.

Rope Sizes:

There are some common rope lengths and sizes in Canyoneering that we use.

These are 60, 120, 200 and 310 feet. Most canyons' rappels will be at or under 200 feet in length.

For canyons where the tallest rappel is 30 feet, I'm not going to bring my 200 ft rope (if I have other options). That's where I would bring 60 feet and a back-up rope that a friend would carry.

To those starting off, I would get two rope sizes (if you can spare the cost): either 2x 200-ft ropes, or either a 120-ft rope AND a 200-ft rope.

The minimum in diameter rappelling rope that you should buy is an 8 mm rope. Even then, this rope is designed for intermediate to experts as this rope is skinnier, lighter, and needs more caution and setup to rappel on it. Heavier people (above 190 lbs.) will most likely not enjoy this rope as you will need more friction to be added to all of your rappels.

And before long, you will need to be buy a pull-cord. I would suggest a 6 mm 200-foot, static rope which also is in a rope bag (an additional cost).

DO NOT buy a dynamic pull-cord rope. They may be cheaper to buy BUT they make a world of a difference when it comes to retrieving the rope. The dynamic pull-cord will stretch and stretch without budging the rappel rope on top! All of that energy you are exerting, will get absorbed by the stretch! So, that means a lot of people pulling down on the pull-cord may not budge the rope at all!

(Lesson learned a long time ago on a rappel that was 220 ft, and we had to hike back to the top to retrieve it).

Rope Types:

There are two primary types of ropes: **Dynamic** & **Static**.
Dynamic ropes are designed to stretch. This stretchiness is what absorbs the energy in case of a fall. It's primarily made of nylon. Dynamic rope is primarily meant for rock-climbers where falls can be common.

Static ropes are primarily designed for strictly rappelling. That's in fact what canyoneers primarily use! Static ropes are not "weaker" or "less strong" than dynamic ropes, but rather serve a different purpose. The goal with static ropes is to offer strength while being *compact* in size. Some canyons require you (or someone who is able!) to carry this rope ALL-DAY. Having been the pack-mule for my group for most of my friend's canyoneering trips, I can indeed say, that having a smaller and lighter rope makes a world of a difference. But the skinnier the rope, the *MORE* friction you will need to add!

Canyoneers typically use ropes that are either 8mm, 8.3 mm, or 9 mm rope sizes. Our pull-cord is the only rope that is 6 mm in size or less. You can rappel on 6mm, but it is in emergency use only because MUCH more friction is needed to rappel safely done. Please DO NOT rappel on 6 mm rope. You or one of your friends will get seriously injured or killed.

Rope Maintenance:

You do not need to be washing and cleaning your brand-new rope at every rappel. If there is a lot of sand in the rope, a rinsing in a pothole of water would be advisable. Otherwise, all of those grains of sand will be embedded in the rope and as people rappel down, that sand will literally act as a type of saw and wear out your descender/rappel device. Even after one rappel. This is especially true with aluminum devices.

Steel descender/rappel devices and carabiners are much more durable when it comes to sand. One steel carabiner, for example, is above $75 and weighs over 0.50 lbs.! It is worth considering if you plan on doing a LOT of slot canyons.

If the rope is wet after your trip and is ready to be stored, let it air dry outside (but not in direct sunlight) for about 30-minutes. You do not want to store it wet for long periods of time.

It's good practice to examine your ropes once before a trip. You are specifically looking for "core-shots" or deep cuts on the rope. If it has light "fuzzing", this is considered acceptable as it is formed when a descender device gets hot (while rappelling) and rubs over the rope.

Additional Reading:
- Ropelabs.au: "Rope Materials"

Rope Terminology

Module 25

When you are talking about knots or ropes, it's important to use its specific terminology and vernacular. Yes, when talking about a singular rope, or multiple ropes, or which part of the rope you are referencing, all matters! Let's take a look below.

Abrasion Zone – The area of a rope that experiences repeated contact with rough surfaces, leading to wear.

Bend – The point where two ropes are joined together with a knot.

Bight – A simple U-shaped bend in the rope that does not cross over itself.

Breakpoint – The weakest spot in a rope where it is most likely to fail under stress.

Core (Kern) – The inner strands of a kernmantle rope that provide most of the rope's strength.

Core Shot – A point of severe damage where the sheath is worn through, exposing the inner core. If you see a core shot in your rope, you need to replace it. Your life may be at risk! If the core-shot is near the end of the rope, you could just simply cut that part off and have a shorter rope. But be hesitant in re-using it as there may be other damage elsewhere that is visible or not.

"Dress the Knot" - a saying and procedure in which the proper arrangement of all the knot parts, which removing unnecessary kinks, twists, and slack, and all rope parts of the knot are touching.

Friction Hitch – A type of knot that tightens when loaded but slides when unweighted, such as a Prusik knot.

Fuzzy Rope – A rope with excessive wear on the sheath, causing fibers to fray outward.

Hard Spot – A stiff or compressed section in a rope, often caused by internal damage or excessive wear.

Hitch – A knot that secures a rope to another object, such as a post.

Knot - a "complication" of the rope that can be used for decorative purposes (such as a bowtie, or tie for a formal meeting, church, job interview, etc.) and practical purposes, such as rappelling, carrying a load, and tying-down objects.

Load Memory – The tendency of a rope to retain bends or kinks after being under tension.

Load Strand – The part of a rope bearing the most weight during use.

Loop – A fully enclosed circle or oval shape made by bending the rope.

"mm" - millimeter for short. This refers to the size, as measured in millimeters, which is the thickness of the rope. The bigger the number, the wider and weight (from more rope material) the rope will be.

Overwrap – When a rope crosses over itself, increasing friction and potential wear.

"Pass the Knot" - a saying in which a rappeller needs to do a bypass at a point of the rappel, such as at a bend (which means, that two ropes were joined together with a knot), and you need to use a technique to bypass that knot so that you can continue rappelling on that rope. This technique requires much practice before doing it in a canyon with real life consequences as you dangle 100 feet up in there, hoping that you re-connect to the rope safely!

Rope Diameter – The thickness of a rope, which affects its strength and handling.

Running End (Working End) – The free-moving end of the rope used to tie knots or make adjustments.

Sheath (Mantle) – The outer protective covering of a kernmantle rope, designed to protect the inner core.

Slack – The portion of the rope that is loose and not under tension.

Splice – A method of permanently joining two rope ends by weaving the fibers together.

Standing End – The fixed or anchored part of the rope that does not move while tying a knot.

Strands – The individual fiber bundles that are twisted together to make a rope.

Tail (Tag End) – The short leftover piece of rope extending beyond a knot.

Tensile Core – The inner fibers of a static rope designed to support heavy loads with minimal stretch.

Tensioned End – The section of rope actively holding weight or force.

Twist (Helix) – The natural spiral shape formed by fibers or strands of rope.

Underwrap – A rope segment that runs beneath another strand, reducing surface contact.

Whipping – A technique used to prevent a rope's end from fraying by binding it with thread or tape.

"Rigging" refers to the way we setup our rappelling systems. The **three** found in canyoneering are:

1) Releasable and Dynamic/Contingency

This allows people to rappel like normal on a single rope, but if a problem was to arise hair gets stuck, unable to rappel further, etc. This allows you to simply convert the rigging to a lowering system WHILE the rope is loaded! In modern days, the word contingency is essentially "what is your backup plan" if "something" happens.

The most common are:

- **Munter Mule** (most used in my experience).
- **Figure-8 Block** (sometimes called Dynamic Figure-8)
- **Totem 8 Block**

THESE ARE NOT COVERED in this book as these needs HANDS-ON practice and an _instructor_ who is experienced in showing how it works. This is where _Professional Instruction_ (aka Guiding Services/Companies) is worth the cost!

2) Rope-Blocked Systems

A rope-blocked system is typically found where a knot (in this book, a clove hitch/triple clove hitch) is used to block off one side of the anchor while you rappel off the other side of the block.

It is VITAL that you know _which side_ to rappel on.

Dozens of accidents have happened because people have rappelled off the wrong side and since there was no rope-block, it was as if they just fell from the top of the rappel! Some lived, others died.

It takes 5 extra seconds to make sure you are rappelling on the blocked side of the rope.

The most common Rope-Blocked system:

- **Clove Hitch/Triple Clove Hitch**

3) Toss N' Go

Toss N' Go is where you go "double strand", which means that there is no rope-block or contingency point involved. It is simply finding the middle of the rope and rappelling on both strands of the rope to the bottom.

This is a very fast way to rappel but does not allow for contingency! If someone's hair gets stuck or something else happens to the rappeller, you will need to deploy a second rope (and hopefully you brought one!) to rescue the person. Toss N' Go is usually setup for small rappels where the "penalty points" isn't high.

Blocking off one of the strands and rappelling on just one isn't a toss n go but has now converted to a rope-blocked system.

My suggestion, if you employ this, is to do this on short rappels, usually under 30 feet, people with long hair show mastery of having their hair tied back, and generally with people who have a mastery of rappelling.

Optional: Courtesy Rigging

A simple technique that essentially eliminates aggressive **rope grooving** (remember the pictures in **Module 7**) at the lip of the edge and can solve 99% of stuck ropes challenges, but there are some caveats. **This is NOT taught in this book**, but please seek **Professional Instruction** on how to set one up and to practice it.

Intro to Rappelling
(w/step-by-step procedure)

As there are numerous "descender devices" out on the market, please read the manual on yours before you do your first rappel. It is CRITICAL to know how to operate yours.

The flow of the rope will be universal as it will take it from the top of the device to the bottom. But the one that you use will depend on what type of friction levels you can start off with or add on the fly.

Before you begin rappelling, first, as a pre-check, make sure that your rope is touching the bottom of the ground. If it's not, readjust the rope length.

Next, realize how high the rappel is and your body weight (which can include a heavy backpack).

After you know how to use your descender device correctly from the manual, use the correct amount of friction for your weight and length of the rappel.

Are you unsure of what friction levels you should be using? Find a local cliff in your neck of the woods and bring at least one experienced person who has rappelled before and let them show you and belay you as you go over the edge for the first time! It's exciting.

Your first canyon trip should not be the first time you have ever rappelled! You will BE a liability for your whole team once they find out that you haven't rappelled before.

Here are some things you can remember for when you first rappel:

- Trust your guide and their knowledge. If something doesn't seem right, say something.

- It's perfectly natural to feel scared or awkward as you lean over the edge. And lean, you must!

- You want to rappel perpendicular to the wall, not parallel or try to climb it.

- Keep your brake hand either by either side of your waist and let the rope feed through.

- You can use a leather glove to absorb some of the friction heat that is given off while you rappel.

  o But it is not mandatory. In fact, the community argues that you should know how to rappel without the aid of a glove as it can create a false sense of security.

- When you are attached to the anchor, remove the extra slack from the rope.

- Slowly walk backwards with the rope feeding through your brake hand.

- When you get to the transition from horizontal ground to vertical wall, this is where you need to lean back and get perpendicular to the wall.

NEVER, EVER, LET GO OF YOUR BRAKING HAND! Even if you feel like your face is going to smash into the wall, don't let go of your hand to protect your face. It's better to have your face smashed-in a bit versus you letting go and essentially free-falling to your death.

When you are in learning how to rappel (while under the supervision of another rappeller), here are some things to keep in mind:

- Don't "bounce" or jump on the rope.
- Don't go side to side, like a pendulum.
- Practice at your comfort level and speed while rappelling.
- Practice adding friction while on rappel with your specific descender device.
- Practice stopping while on rappel and locking-off.

If there is a cliff edge that is just too much or too scary to walk off, a STRONG recommendation is to literally sit on the ground near the edge and scoot your butt off slowly. I've done this once early in my rappelling days and it worked great. This is called a "sit start".

Learning these steps can significantly improve your rappelling skills and turn it into an enjoyable experience.

It has been said that rappelling while canyoneering is not the reason why we do it and I tend to agree. However, rappelling is a very fun part of the experience, but it should not be the primary purpose, in my humble opinion. A secondary reason, sure.

#1 - Harness on.

#2 - Helmet on.

#3 - Attach PAS to Harness

#4 - Attach PAS via <u>Girth Hitch</u> to belay loop (or another loop adjacent to belay loop).

#5 - Attach Carabiner to PAS

#6 - Attach Carabiner to Gear Loop (to keep out of the way).

#7 - Attach descender device to carabiner, which is then attached to the belay loop

#8 - Attach 3x carabiners to gear loop on harness.

#9 - Locate anchors at rappel (if any).

#10 - 1st thing - "clip in" via your PAS to the anchor (so you don't slip off the wall while you are setting up the rappel!)

#11 - PAS in this picture is clipped into the chains

#12 - Get rappel ready. Bring rappel rope close to anchor.

#13 - Thread rappel rope through quick link (or what is appropriate for your rappel station and anchor)

#14 - Yell "Rope!" or "hey! heads up - I'm tossing a rope down" - followed by tossing the rope(bag) down.

#15 - Setup your rappelling knot (it depends for each rappel, your group situation/dynamics, if there is a water flow, etc.)

#16 - Thread rope through your rappel device

#17 - See the slack from the rappel device to the anchor?

#18 - Remove slack by pushing extra rope through rappel device

#19 - Last; remove PAS from anchor point.

#20 - Get feet firmly planted on rock wall.

#21 - Legs should be perpendicular to wall; keep brake-hand by waist.

#22 - Walk backwards down the wall, maintaining good friction control.

#23 (Angle from the bottom looking up at the rappeller)

#24 - Good technique here; It should "look" this way when you (or someone else) are rappelling.

#25 - Bad technique being demonstrated here; don't try to climb-down. Rappel! And Rappel with your legs out. It's much easier and less scary than you might think.

#26 - Similar as before, not good technique, but slightly better. Can you see the slightly improved technique? You want to become nearly perpendicular with the wall; not like the previous photo.

#27 - At an overhang, first, plant your feet right at edge, while staying perpendicular.

#28 - Feet are still on ledge, but lower your butt/upper half, LOWER than your legs.

#29 - Butt/upper half is nearly at the stretch point for Sarah. Good technique for safely rappelling an overhang.

#30 - When you can't lower butt/upper half anymore, drag feet off of cliff edge.

#31 - Doing it this way, prevents your head from hitting the rock wall and minimizes swinging/bouncing on the rope (which increases the force that is exerted on the anchor above).

#32 - Sarah is now ready to rappel again, and with hair, fingers, and gear away from rock wall.

#33 - Sarah continuing with the rappel

#34 - Nearly at the bottom of the rappel!

#35 - Reached the bottom! Rope and descender device STILL attached at bottom of rappel

#36 - Depending on your rappel device, you may remove the rope from the device while the descender device is STILL attached to your harness. This is good practice and a standard, as it minimizes dropping the device in water or a water-filled pothole, where it may be impossible to retrieve!

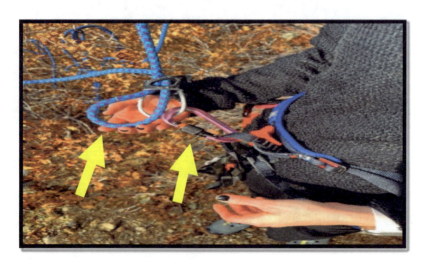

#37 - Rope almost removed from descender device.

#38 - Rope, now removed completely. Descender device still attached to harness. All done! Nicely done Sarah!

Step-by-Step

Step 1: Secure Your PAS
Before doing anything else, clip your Personal Anchor System (PAS) to a quick link or webbing at the anchor. This keeps you securely attached to the anchor and prevents fatal falls if you slip.

Step 2: Set up the Rope
With your PAS secured, prepare the rappel rope. Choose the appropriate rigging method—releasable (ghosting), contingency, single strand, or double strand—based on the plan. Attach the pull-cord if using one and confirm the setup with your group or guide.

Step 3: Drop the Rope
Drop the rope over the edge while staying attached with your PAS. Toss it carefully.

Step 4: Check the Rope
Ensure the rope reaches the bottom. Listen for a thud if you are using a rope bag, or visually confirm. If the rope is snagged or does not reach, pull it back up and re-toss. Stay clipped in and look over the edge if needed.

Step 5: Verify the Knot
Inspect the knot securing the rope to the anchor. Ensure it is tied correctly, snug, and secure before continuing.

Step 6: Thread the Rope
Thread the rope through your descender device. Right-handed individuals should keep the rope in their right hand and outside their right foot; left-handed individuals should do the same on their left side.

Step 7: Remove Slack
Pull out any excess slack in the rope from the descender device to the anchor point. This ensures a smooth rappel start.

Step 8: Detach Your PAS

When ready to rappel, unclip your PAS from the anchor. Keep a secure grip on the rope to maintain control.

Step 9: Maintain a Brake Head

Always keep your brake hand at waist level, away from the descender device, to control the rope.

Step 10: Position Yourself

With your feet firmly on the rock, lean back, and create a perpendicular stance. This creates stability to start from.

Step 11: Begin Rappelling

Walk backward down the wall, maintaining control with your brake hand. Tighten your grip to slow down or loosen it slightly to descend faster.

Step 12: Monitor Friction

Adjust your friction settings during the descent, particularly on long rappels. This helps you maintain controlled movement.

Step 13: Landing (last step)

Once you reach the bottom, leave your descender device attached to your harness if possible. Remove only the rope portion to prevent dropping or losing the device.

Intro to Ascending

Module 28

Basic Procedure for Rope Ascending:

 1. **Preparation**: Ensure your ascending system includes a top-handled ascender and a foot loop or secondary ascender. Check all equipment for wear and tear before starting.

 2. **Attachment**: Clip the top-handled ascender onto the rope and secure your harness to it with a locking carabiner. Attach a foot loop to the ascender or use a secondary ascender for additional support.

 3. **Movement Technique**: Push the top ascender upward until it locks, then stand in the foot loop to lift yourself. Slide the bottom or secondary ascender up to reset your position. Repeat the motion in a steady rhythm, using your legs for most of the work to reduce arm fatigue.

Pro Tips:
Practice First: Ascending is physically demanding; train on a static rope in a controlled environment before attempting in a canyon.

Carry a Backup: Always have a secondary system like a Prusik or an autoblock for added safety. Ascending may not be used often but mastering it can save your life or prevent a trip from turning into a rescue.

This is NOT entirely taught in this book/website as this is a very Hands-on practice that should be should by a qualified instructor or canyoneering leader.

Sequencing (or moving) in a canyon

Module 29

"Why is there a section on 'moving in a canyon'? Don't you just hike or walk through one?

The answer lies in understanding the unique challenges every canyon presents. Remember, every canyon is unique!

Moving through a canyon isn't just hiking—it's about how you navigate it. You will be hiking (for most of it), but you will also be downclimbing, upclimbing, stemming, chimneying, bridging, using handlines, jumping, or even working with your team for partner assists. These different techniques are forms of **"sequencing."**

Each canyon contains a mix of these skills, which adds to the canyon adventure, which I love! This variety is what makes canyoneering so much fun—it's the 'spice' of the canyon experience, as I often say to beginners.

Here they all are:

- Downclimbing
- Upclimbing
- Stemming
- Chimneying
- Bridging
- Handline
- Jumping
- Partner Assist

Downclimbing

Upclimbing

Stemming

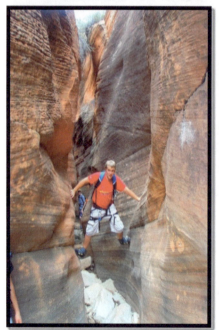 

Chimneying

Bridging

Handline

Jumping

Partner Assist

Unit 3: "Advanced Canyoneering" Overview

Modules 30 - 36

Advanced canyoneering pushes the limits of technical skills, requiring precision, creativity, and teamwork to navigate extreme challenges. Techniques like releasable anchors, ghosting, progress capture, and pothole escapes are just the beginning. Success in advanced canyons demands preparation, practice, appropriate canyon gear and experienced team members.

Most of these things will NOT be taught here in this book, but these concepts are meant for **professional training**.

Key Challenges:

- **Rescue Scenarios**: Responding to emergencies, such as incapacitated teammates or stuck rappellers, requires advanced rigging techniques, improvisation, and calm decision-making under pressure.
- **Big/Tall Rappels**: Descents over 200 feet demand precise friction control to manage rope heat and speed. Strategies include using advanced rappel devices, dangling a backpack from the harness to improve balance and reduce strain, and practicing extended rappel techniques.
- **Passing a Knot on Rappel**: For long descents requiring multiple ropes, the ability to safely and smoothly transition past a knot is critical. This involves precise rigging, situational awareness, and proficiency rappelling devices.
- **Keeper Potholes**: Deep, wide potholes (potentially filled with water) require advanced escape methods like teamwork, specialized gear (e.g., sandbags), and creative problem-solving.

- **Ghosting**: A leave-no-trace approach that demands innovative rigging methods like sand or water anchors to preserve the canyon environment.
- **Mae West**: an extremely committing maneuver where a canyoneer must stem 20-50 feet above a narrow slot, relying on strength, flexibility, and body tension to stay suspended. A slip can result in serious injury or death, as falling into the tight canyon below could lead to entrapment, broken bones, or fatal impact with the rock walls and ground.
- **Hair Entanglement**: Scenarios like hair getting jammed in a rappel device are potentially life-threatening. Solutions depend on available gear, such as a second rope, or improvisation when gear is limited. Prevention (e.g., securing hair under a helmet) is vital.
- **Packrafting**: Necessary for certain canyons, like those in the Grand Canyon, packrafting combines water navigation after canyon exploration. Skills in swift water techniques and hauling large amounts of gear (and weight) are essential.

Why Professional Training Matters? Exposure to these techniques is no substitute for hands-on instruction. Advanced scenarios often carry high risks, and incorrect execution can lead to severe consequences. Seek professional training through organizations like the American Canyoneering Association (ACA) to develop the confidence and competence needed for safe canyon navigation.

Progressing in Canyoneering

Module 30

After completing initial canyons, many canyoneers feel drawn to more challenging adventures. While this is natural, overestimating your abilities or underestimating the canyon can lead to dangerous situations. Each canyon is unique, demanding specific skills, gear, and preparation. Advanced canyons often require 12–16+ hour days, including taxing approaches and exits, leaving canyoneers physically and mentally exhausted.

Physical and Mental Demands:

- **Exhaustion**: Long canyons require heavy packs (30–50 lbs.) with essential gear, such as ropes, webbing, and rescue tools. Exit hikes in darkness, dehydration, and fatigue can test even seasoned canyoneers.
- **Solitude**: Remote canyons are often isolated, seeing few visitors, which means rescue may be days away. Self-sufficiency is essential.

Key Challenges in Advanced Canyons, Examples:

- **Complex Obstacles**: Keeper potholes, extended high stemming, and technical rappels demand advanced skills.
- **Big/Tall Rappels**: Descents over 300 feet require precise friction control, managing rope heat, and creative rigging, like attaching heavy backpacks to the harness for balance.
- **Passing a Knot on Rappel**: Safely transitioning past a rope join is crucial for long descents and demands proficiency with specialized techniques and backups.
- **Rescue Scenarios**: Handling emergencies such as stuck rappelers, stuck hair in a descender device, or equipment failure requires advanced problem-solving and teamwork.

Advanced canyons may require tools such as aiders, sandtraps, toggles, and pothole escape gear, along with mastery of techniques like ghosting, rigging releasable anchors, and natural anchor systems. Many of these challenges fall under "V" canyons with "R" or "X" ratings, indicating high risk or extreme physical demands.

To safely progress:
- **Partner with Experts**: Join experienced teams for your first advanced canyons.
- **Thorough Research**: Study each canyon's unique obstacles and logistics (and know that they can change).
- **Professional Instruction**: Learn from qualified organizations like the American Canyoneering Association (ACA) to develop essential skills in a hands-on setting.

Canyoneering is as much about preparation as an adventure too. The challenges of advanced canyons will push you to your physical and mental limits.

Here are some snippets from the website **American Canyoneers Association**, "Skills Checklists," that you can freely download to see how you would progress and perfect your canyoneering skills in a formal setting. Their classes are taught where a hands-on course would take place by an ACA qualified leader.

Core Skills Courses:
- Sovereign Canyoneer Course
- Aspirant Course
- Aspirant Canyon Leader Course
- Canyon Leader Course
- Canyon Rescue Course
- Assistant Pro Guide
- Lead Pro Guide

Recreational Canyoner:
- Core
- Sovereign Canyoneer

Recreational Canyon Leader:
- Aspirant
- Assistant Canyon Leader
- Canyon Leader

Pro Canyon Guide:
- Single Site Pro Canyon Guide
- Assistant Pro Canyon Guide
- Lead Pro Canyon Guide
- Master Canyon Guide

Down below, you will see glimpses of the advanced training that the ACA provides to its students.

Navigation, Map Reading, Canyon Topos
Read contour lines on a topographic map; identify terrain features (hills, saddles, ridges, drainages), determine relative steepness of grade, identify potential high ground and canyon escape routes.
Identify relative size of a canyon watershed using topo map.

Problem Solving Scenarios
Scenario 1: Shirt / Hair stuck in rappelling device.
Scenario 2: Tangled roped and/or rope doesn't touch the ground.
Scenario 3: Late start - move group expeditiously.
Scenario 4: Horizontal Evacuation of lower leg injury - stable patient; normal conditions.

On Rope Techniques, Companion Rescue

Ascend a fixed rope using friction hitches; single strand, double strand.

Ascend a fixed rope using mechanical ascenders; single strand.

Transition from rappel to ascend and from ascend to rappel.

Pass a knot while rappelling. Pass a knot while ascending.

Demonstrate rappelling on a Guided Rappel (set up by a competent person). Explain safety concerns and mitigation.

Rescue Rigging and Rescue

Describe and demonstrate an understanding of how various rigging and belay systems can facilitate or hinder rescue.

Convert static twin rope rigging (e.g stone knot) to lower. Use hands free backup (i.e. friction hitch) when lowering.

Convert tail-up rigging (e.g. fiddlestick) to lower utilizing rescue rope. Use hands free backup (i.e. friction hitch) when lowering.

Perform a pick-off rescue of a person stuck on rope utilizing a second rescue rope, including the use of a self-belay.

Perform a pick-off rescue of a person stuck on rope without utilizing a second rescue rope, descending the subject's tensioned rope. Include the use of a self-belay.

Intro to Anchors and Rigging

Evaluate and rig existing fixed artificial anchors (bolts) using the acronym EARNEST (Equalized, Angle, Redundant, No Extension, Strong, Timely).

Identify, Evaluate, and rig single-point natural anchors (i.e. tree, boulder, arch) using a) simple webbing wrap, b) cinching wrap (i.e. wrap 2 pull 1, Girth hitch).
Explain the pros and cons of each and demonstrate how to securely back up & test single point anchors.

Set up and use a releasable/contingency system for rappel. Explain the hazards/risks of using releasable systems and steps that should be taken to avoid accidents and mitigate risks.

See more information at:

https://www.canyoneering.net/resources/

Rigging for Releaseable

Module 31

This page is to briefly cover what it means "**rig for releasable**" but there is NO expectation for you to practice it or do it as it is considered part of Advanced Canyoneering. Rigging for releasable allows a rope anchor to be safely *retrieved* after use, minimizing environmental impact and preserving resources. This method is essential in "ghosting" canyons, where no permanent anchors are left behind. While it's an advanced technique, understanding its basics helps beginner canyoneers progress safely and responsibly.

Practice only in a controlled environment and with an experienced guide.

Procedure:
1. **Anchor Setup**: Attach the rope to a stable natural anchor, like a tree, rock, or sandbag.
2. **Releasable Device**: Use "toggles" such as a fiddlestick, totem, or smooth operator, which can be controlled remotely via a 2nd or 3rd rope.
3. **Backup**: Always include a safety backup, like tying the rope to a carabiner or friction hitch, to prevent premature release during descent.
4. **Test Before Use**: Gently load the anchor to confirm it's secure and will release smoothly.
5. **Rope Retrieval**: After the first team member descends, pull the rope gently but firmly to see if the "toggle" could release. But don't do it. Just verify. If not, adjust the system and try again.

Pros of Releasable Rigging:

- **Minimal Environmental Impact**: Leaves no permanent traces, maintaining the canyon's pristine state.
- **Efficiency**: Reduces the need for extra rope or equipment.
- **Emergency Flexibility**: A stuck or jammed rope can sometimes be resolved by releasing the system remotely.

Cons of Releasable Rigging:

- **Higher Risk**: Misjudging the system can lead to anchor failure or rope loss (getting stuck).
- **Complexity**: Requires precision and practice to rig correctly.
- **Not Always Suitable**: Some canyon conditions (e.g., poor anchor points, high friction) make this method impractical.

Tips for Beginners:

- **Learn from Experts**: Practice under the guidance of a skilled canyoneer or instructor.
- **Practice on Easy Terrain**: Before applying in advanced canyons, test releasable setups in controlled environments.
- **Know the Tools**: Understand and practice using releasable devices: toggles, ropes, and knots.
- **Inspect Anchors**: Always verify the strength and stability of the natural anchor before trusting it with your weight.

Photography in Slot Canyons
Module 32

Challenges with Light and Contrast:
Photographing slot canyons is notoriously difficult due to the stark contrast between the bright sky above and the deep shadows below. While our eyes adapt seamlessly, cameras often fail to capture this balance, making images feel underwhelming compared to the experience.

Processing vs. Reality:
Many striking canyon photos are "processed", enhancing colors, contrast, and vibrancy to highlight features like red rock walls or turquoise water. This post-editing, often called "photoshopping," transforms the image into an artistic interpretation rather than a *direct* representation. These edits can create unrealistic expectations for canyon explorers who may find the actual scene less vivid or dramatic. Ask me about how a friend was SEVERELY disappointed when he saw all of these vivid photos of the Subway in Zion, just to be in "meh" after seeing it in person. He was pretty bummed!

Tips for Better Slot Canyon Photography:
- **Use HDR (High Dynamic Range)**: Combine multiple exposures to balance the highlights and shadows.
- **Shoot in RAW**: This file format retains more detail, allowing for better post-processing.
- **Bring a Tripod**: Slot canyons often require longer exposures due to low light. A steady camera is essential.
- **Timing is Key**: Shoot during midday when sunlight filters into the slots, creating dramatic beams and reflections.
- **Be Realistic**: Embrace the natural beauty of canyons rather than striving to replicate processed photos.

Canyoneering First-Aid

Module 33

Canyoneering often takes place in remote, rugged environments where medical assistance may be hours or days away. Proper first-aid knowledge and preparation are critical for handling injuries, illnesses, and emergencies.

First-Aid Kit Essentials:
- **Bandages and Dressings**: Adhesive bandages, gauze pads, medical tape, and elastic bandages for cuts, scrapes, and sprains.
- **Wound Care Supplies**: Antiseptic wipes, antibiotic ointment, tweezers (for splinters or debris), and irrigation syringes.
- **Blister Care**: Moleskin, hydrogel pads, and blister-specific bandages.
- **Medications**: Pain relievers (ibuprofen or acetaminophen), antihistamines, and anti-inflammatory medications.
- **Splinting Materials**: Lightweight, packable splints or SAM splints for fractures or severe sprains.
- **Thermal Protection**: Emergency blanket or bivy sack for hypothermia; fire starter of some kind

Bleeding:
- Apply direct pressure with a clean dressing.
- Elevate the wound (if appropriate) to reduce blood flow.
- Secure with gauze and tape.
- For severe bleeding, use a tourniquet as a last resort.

Fractures or Sprains:
- Immobilize the injured area with a splint or improvised materials.
- Avoid moving the person unless absolutely necessary.
- Use cold packs (or canyon water) to reduce swelling.

Hypothermia:
- Remove wet clothing and insulate the person with dry materials.
- Use an emergency blanket or bivy sack to retain heat.
- Offer warm fluids if the person is conscious and able to drink.

Dehydration or Heat Exhaustion:
- Rehydrate with water or electrolyte solutions.
- Move to a shaded, cooler area and rest.
- Cool the body with wet clothes or immersion in water.

Snake Bites or Allergic Reactions:
- Keep the bite area immobilized and lower than the heart.
- Administer an antihistamine or epinephrine if necessary for allergic reactions.
- Seek professional medical help immediately.

Tips for Beginners:
- **Take a Wilderness First-Aid Course**: Wilderness first-aid training prepares you for remote scenarios.
- **Pack Compactly**: A lightweight, waterproof first-aid kit ensures you're prepared without adding unnecessary bulk.
- **Group Responsibility**: Distribute first-aid supplies among the group to share the load.
- **Know Emergency Protocols**: Be familiar with the canyon's exit routes and ensure someone in the group has a satellite phone or alternative.

Mastering Pothole Escapes

Potholes and keeper potholes are natural depressions in canyons that can trap water, debris, or even canyoneers (unfortunately). Successfully "conquering" them requires specialized skills, tools, and teamwork. These obstacles test both problem-solving and physical abilities, making them a hallmark of advanced canyoneering.

Understanding the Unique Challenges:

- **Potholes**: Bowl-shaped features that may hold water and require creative techniques to exit.
- **Keeper Potholes**: Deeper and more challenging to escape, often with undercut edges or slick walls, designed to "keep" you inside. Not all potholes are created equally! Each canyon that contains one (or many) will be uniquely different and challenging. Even when you go can affect the pothole situation (dry, filled-up after a rainstorm, or half-way full and can't touch the bottom).

Essential Techniques:

- **Boosts and Partner Assists**: Using team members to help climb out.
- **Pack Tosses**: Throwing weighted packs over the pothole lip for leverage.
- **Deadman Anchors**: Creating anchors using rocks, sand, or bags.
- **Mechanical Advantage Systems**: Consider using pulleys to increase lifting power.

Key Gear/Tools:

- **Potshot Bags**: Fabric bags filled with sand or rocks for weight and thrown to create anchors.

- **Ropes and Ascenders**: For climbing out of deep potholes (see next page for graphic).
- **Etriers** (Ladders): Lightweight webbing steps for added height (see next page for graphic).
- **Pulleys and Carabiners**: To create haul systems for difficult exits.
- **Wetsuits** or **Dry Suits**: For prolonged exposure in cold water-filled potholes.
- **Packraft** or **pool toys**: Bringing a blowup pool toy would allow a person to float above the water.

<u>Safety and Teamwork</u>:
- **Pre-Plan Strategies**: Assess obstacles and plan exits before committing.
- **Communicate Clearly**: Ensure everyone understands the approach and gameplan.
- **Conserve Energy**: Potholes can be exhausting! Use efficient techniques and rotate responsibilities.

Not only do you need to equip yourself with the right skills, tools, and mindset to tackle these challenges, but the rest of your team needs to be up to par too.

Handled Ascenders

Etriers

"Canyoneering Emergency Note"

Module 35

Leaving an **emergency note** in your vehicle is a simple yet critical step for enhancing safety during a canyoneering adventure. This note provides vital information to local Search and Rescue (SAR) teams in case of an emergency.

Here's what to include:

1. **Trip Details**: The size of your group (total number of participants). (Optional: First names, if comfortable) Emergency contact information for group leader the name(s) of the canyon(s) you plan to explore and first time/not familiar or familiar with area. Any known medical conditions or allergies within the group.

2. **Timing and Schedule**: Date and time the canyon adventure began. Anticipated return time to the vehicle.

3. **Additional Notes**: Mention any alternate plans, such as potential exit routes or backup canyons.

This form (on the next page) can be photocopied (or found online on canyoneering101.com) and kept on hand for multiple trips. Place the completed note clearly visible on your vehicle's dashboard before starting your canyon.

By doing this **optional** task, you empower SAR teams to locate and assist you more effectively in case of an emergency.

Canyoneering Emergency Note

What Canyon(s)?

_____

Who is the Trip leader and phone number:

_____

First time/Repeat adventure?

_____

How many people are in your group?

_____

When do you plan on Starting and Finishing?

_____

Emergency Contact w/Phone Number:

_____

Known medical concerns/allergies?

_____

Alternate Exit Plans/Backup Canyons?

_____

To Fill in the Gaps...

Module 36

Hiking and canyoneering are great opportunities to bond with your group. Use the time to engage in light, fun, and/or meaningful conversations that can **pass the hours** and strengthen connections and trust.

Here are a few topics to keep in the back of your head:

Get to Know Each Other:
Start with personal stories. Ask about each other's backgrounds, where they're from, and what brought them to canyoneering. Sharing experiences can create a relaxed, enjoyable, and personable atmosphere.

Favorite Stories:
Everyone has memorable stories. Share funny, scary, or inspiring adventures you've had on past hikes or canyoneering trips. These tales can build camaraderie and laughter.

Other Hobbies:
Discuss hobbies beyond hiking and canyoneering. From cooking to photography or even unique interests like collecting rocks or bird watching, learning about others' passions at the minimum passes the time, but also grows comradery and trust within the group. Also, you may find out that - hey, we are not so different from each other after all.

Canyoneering Experience:
Ask how long they've been canyoneering, and what they've learned over the years. Share tips and advice, especially if you or they are all seasoned explorers or new to the sport.

Space, Science, and the Universe:
For those who enjoy deep discussions, dive into space exploration, recent scientific discoveries, or theories about the universe. These topics can spark fascinating debates or moments of awe.

Politics, Religion, and Meaning of Life:
If the group is comfortable, explore weightier topics like politics, religion, or the meaning of life. Be mindful of each person's preferences — keep it respectful and open.

These conversations not only help pass time but also (hopefully) create stronger bonds within the group, making the canyon experience even more memorable. Who knows - maybe this new group will be your "new" canyoneering friends' group? Or maybe you will get invited to more canyoneering trips? (Or, maybe you won't? But you at least will possibly know why!)

Canyoneering Knots

Webbing (What is it?)

Overhand Knot

Water Knot

Figure-8 Knot

Figure-8 – On a Bight

Figure-8 – Follow-through

Clove Hitch/Triple Clove Hitch

Munter Hitch

Girth Hitch

Stone Hitch

European Death Knot (EDK)

Double-Fisherman Bend

Figure 8 Bend

Webbing (What Is It?)

Webbing is what lays the foundation for rappelling anchors. While it has other secondary uses, creating reliable, safe anchors is its primary usage.

You can buy webbing "by the foot" from climbing stores, allowing you to customize lengths.

There are two main types:

- **flat webbing** - a flat, high-tensile strength nylon, and;
- **tubular webbing** - which is more durable than flat webbing, providing additional strength but it is more costly.

"**Flat webbing**" is just a pattern of weaved nylon fibers that has a high-tensile strength! Due to the nature of it being flat, if it gets dragged across an edge or sharp rocks its stiffness allows it to tear. Not too easily, but enough to cause everyone to "inspect" it every time at every rappel.

"**Tubular webbing**" is similar to "flat webbing" but uses a tube that lies flat but has the benefits of having the wrap-around webbing as it increases the strength. SterlingRope.com says that one-inch tubular webbing has a minimum breaking strength of 4000-lbs per inch. It can be bought with a higher-rating up to 9800-lbs per inch.

Webbing is made primarily out of nylon, though you may find blends like 90% nylon and 10% polyester. While Kevlar versions exist, they're pricey and unnecessary for canyoneering needs.

The community recommendations are 1 inch (25 mm), and earth-tone colors like black, brown, or tan are preferred for blending in with the natural landscape. Bright colors, like blue or red, should be avoided - they stand out too much and can "ruin" a pristine canyon experience or photo.

Webbing is strong when used properly but needs to be checked frequently for wear, especially after being exposed to sun or water, which can weaken it. It's a good idea to inspect your webbing at each rappel, looking for fraying, cracks, or brittleness, and replace it if necessary. When it doubts, replace it! This your life you we are talking about. It's worth the whole extra two minutes to replace it.

Remember, that canyon conditions change frequently! And you will need to rebuild anchors (a lot!). Don't ASSUME that a water knot is safe just because it's laying there. Examine it! Being in the sun all day will make it brittle and reduce its overall strength. And webbing that's been submerged all day (and for many weeks) will need to be changed as well.

In canyoneering, when you come up to a cliff or drop that needs to be rappelled, you will look for "natural anchors" (such as rocks, boulders, trees, roots, etc.) or fixed ("man-made") anchors to tie your webbing around. The "Water Knot" is the knot that you will be tying your webbing around for these anchors.

Pros:
- Essential, strong, and inexpensive when bought in bulk.

Cons:
- You will be replacing this often so cost can add up. But I see that as a "price to play".

Caution:
- Webbing must be examined at every rappel, every time.
- Look for frayed, cracked, stiff, cut, sun-bleached webbing. Replace it with a new strand.

Recommended Length: 30 feet/person

Recommended Colors: "Earth-tone" IE Black, Brown, Tan. NOT Red, Orange, Blue, Green, etc.

Recommended Width-Size: 1-inch width (or 25 mm)

Canyoneering Usage Examples:
When you encounter a drop without visible anchors, you'll use webbing to sling (wrap around) a "natural anchor" like a tree or boulder, securing it with a Water Knot to create a safe rappelling setup.

Additional Reading:
- Wikipedia.org: "Webbing"
- RopeWiki.com: "Webbing on bolt hangers"
- RopeWiki.com: "Webbing harness"
- DyeClan.com: "Webbing"
- Canyoneering.net: "Webbing Knotcraft"
- Canyoneering.net: "EDK in Webbing?"

Overhand Knot

The **Overhand Knot** is like the ABCs of canyoneering knots - it's simple, foundational, and helps you build/learn upon more complex knots down the line. Think of it as the "building bock" for essential knots like the Water Knot, EDK, and Double Fisherman's Bend - all heavily used in canyoneering.

Pros:
- Serves as the basis for many other knots and is very easy to tie.
- Can be tied quickly and used as a simple stopper knot (in some situations: can't see the bottom; kid rappeler, etc.)

Cons:
- Not strong enough for load-bearing applications; it's more of a building block knot.
- Not strong enough to rappel on its own

Caution:
- Do NOT rappel using this knot; it's not reliable for critical loads (or force).

Canyoneering Usage Examples:
- Used to build other knots such as the Water Knot, EDK, Double-Fisherman Bend.
- Tied as a stopper knot at the end of a rappel rope to prevent accidental descent off the rope's end.
- Used to secure loose ends of a rope or to back up a primary knot, such as a Figure 8 Follow-Through, in anchor systems.

Additional Reading:
- Wikipedia.com: "Overhand Knot"
- AnimatedKnots.com: "Overhand Knot"
- YouTube: "Canyons & Crags: An Overhand is an Overhand Not"

To begin, you will be working with one end of the rope

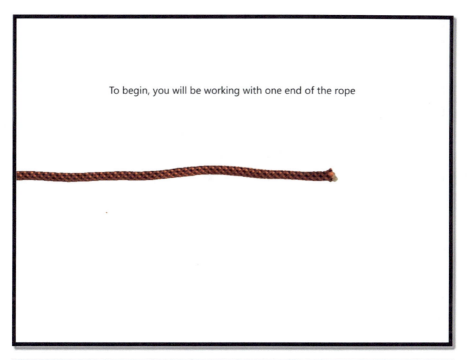

Next, make a loop at the end of the rope

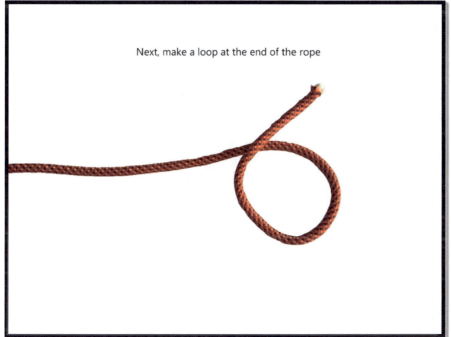

Put the tail end of the rope through the
bottom of the loop and out the top

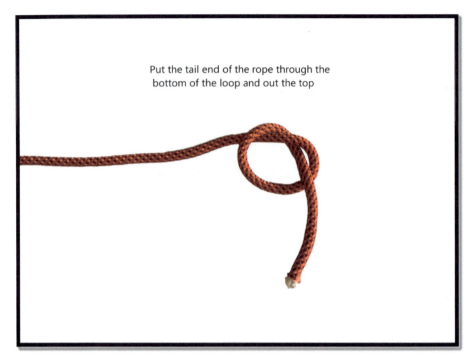

Pull the end of the rope to "dress the knot"

Water Knot

The **Water Knot** (also known as Ring Bend, Grass Knot, or Overhand Follow-through) is a MUST-KNOW knot in canyoneering. It's primarily used to join one end of webbing to the other end, whether you are using a single piece of webbing or two pieces. Since webbing is a staple in canyoneering, you'll be using this knot a lot, so get used to it.

When you come across a cliff or drop that requires rappelling, you'll tie your webbing around natural anchors (rocks, trees, boulders) or fixed (man-made") anchors using the Water Knot. However, always check your knots - canyon conditions do change, and the webbing can get brittle from sun exposure or waterlogged from flashfloods or constant rain. Look for cuts, abrasions, discoloration, and ensure the tails of the webbing strands are at LEAST 3 inches long.

The Water Knot is quite simple to tie and everyone in your group should know how to tie this.

Pros:
- Highly effective for joining webbing; ideal for anchors in canyoneering.
- It is safe to rappel on!
- It is easily identifiable by most canyoneers.

Cons:
- Requires careful dressing and sufficient tails of a minimum of 3" in length
- It is said about the knot that after each rappel, the tail becomes a little shorter.
- Eventually it will need to be retied (which is okay!)
- Hard to untie. If you are having to untie it, using a knife to cut the webbing maybe be faster.

Caution:
- Leave three inches of tail on both strands of the water knot. Any more than 6 inches is unnecessary.
- Just like webbing, check every water knot, every rappel, every time. And when it doubts - just rebuild it! It takes literally two extra minutes to tie it correctly.
- Replace webbing if it looks cracked, cut, has abrasion marks, brittle, stiff, or sun-bleached.

Canyoneering Usage Examples:
- Joining two pieces of webbing to create a sling for an anchor or rappel station.
- Building an improvised harness with webbing in emergencies when a commercial harness is unavailable (or someone forgot theirs or lost it in the canyon!)

Additional Reading:
- Wikipedia.com: "Water knot"
- CanyoneeringUSA.com: "How to Tie a Water Knot and Build a Webbing Anchor"
- DyeClan.com: "Water Knot (Tape Knot)"

How to Tie using ONE strand of webbing

To tie the "Water Knot", you need to start with either end of the webbing.

It's best practice to leave 3" of tail, minimum, once it is complete.

This will show the Water Knot using only one piece of webbing.

In this same module, or later on in the pictures, you will see the Water Knot using two pieces of webbing.

With either end of the webbing, tie an overhand knot.
(I like to go under the webbing and through the hole on top).

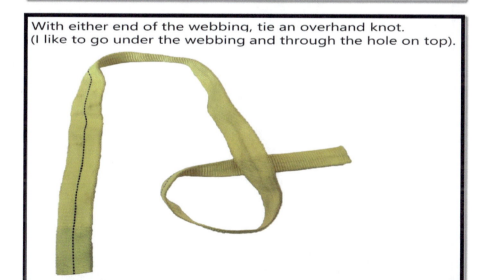

And here is the webbing going through the hole on top, which nearly completes the Overhand Knot.

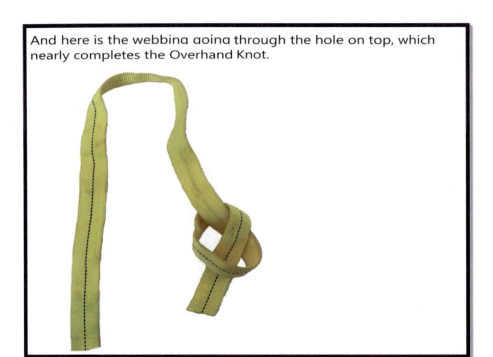

"Dress the Knot" BUT loosely. (Do not make it snug, yet). We are NOT quite done constructing the knot.

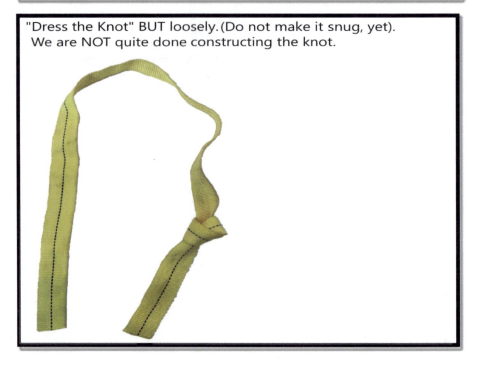

With the OTHER end of the webbing (and to complete the Water Knot) you will be "rethreading" the Overhand Knot IN REVERSE.

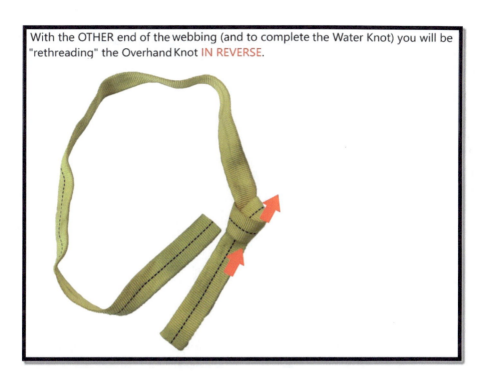

Here, the webbing is threaded under the loop as it continues its journey.

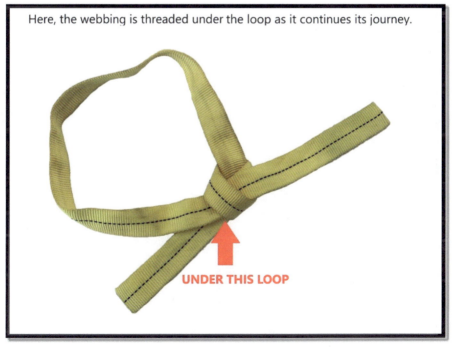

UNDER THIS LOOP

The webbing is retracing the webbing, but in reverse. Here, the webbing is going behind the other webbing and will be brought to the front.

The webbing is following the webbing path, but in reverse.

In the next step, the webbing end will go under both loops (where the arrow is) and out the other end.

Remember to leave about 3" of tail, minimum, at the conclusion of the knot.

Here, the webbing has been "rethreaded" and the end piece is through, thus completing the "Water Knot".

Summary - One Overhand Knot. followed by another Overhand Knot in reverse.

One end of webbing

The other end of webbing

Finally, "Dress the Knot". (Pull snug on either side of the knot).

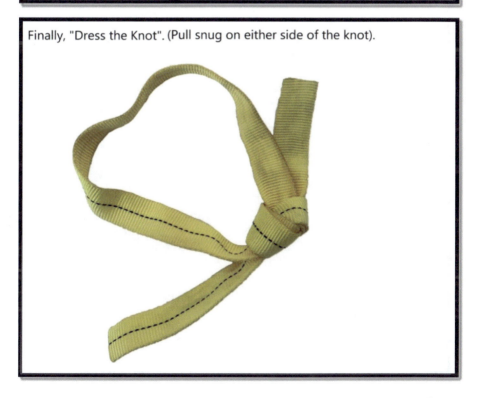

How to Tie using TWO strands of webbing

This is how to tie the Water Knot using <u>two pieces of webbing</u>. (It is the same as if you were tying it on one piece).

This is a visual aid to help you perfect this knot.

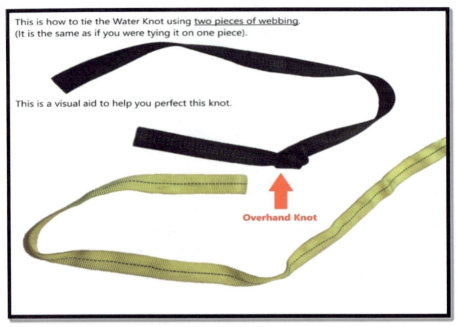

Overhand Knot

"Rethread" the Overhand Knot.

Here, follow the Yellow webbing's path.

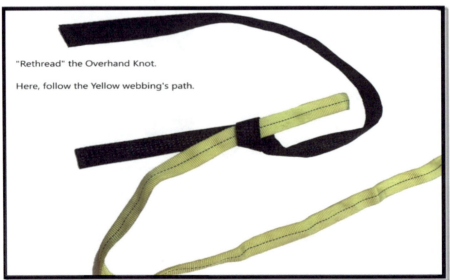

Following the black webbing Overhand Knot's path.

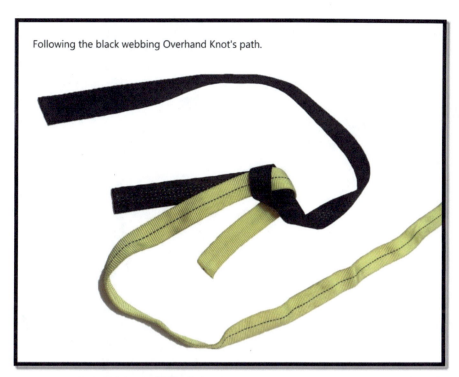

In the next step, the yellow webbing will be going around the knot and then under those loops.

Around the black webbing

Through the yellow loop

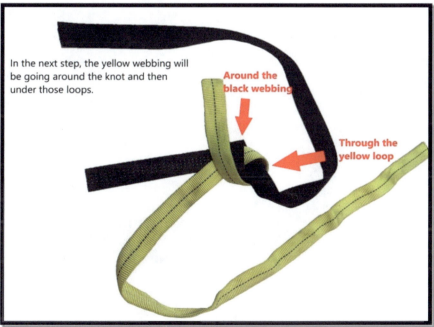

Here, the yellow webbing was "rethreaded", in reverse, on the overhand knot that was tied on the black webbing.

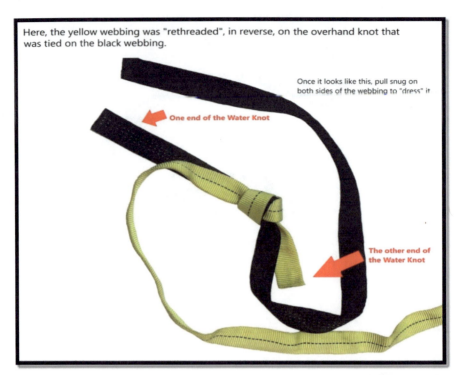

Once it looks like this, pull snug on both sides of the webbing to "dress" it

One end of the Water Knot

The other end of the Water Knot

Here is the other side of Water Knot, using two pieces of webbing.

Figure-8 Knot

The **Figure-8 Knot** is used in Canyoneering primarily for creating a "load carrying" loop. Once tied correctly, you can attach a carabiner to it (by using the Figure 8 Knot on a bight) and then use that to clip it into things such as harnesses (or use the Figure-8 Follow-through knot), anchors, or items (such as to raise/lower things).

This stopper knot is the same as a Figure 8 Follow-through, however, this by itself, is more of a "stopper knot". In canyoneering, these are sometimes used as stopper knots - which is tied at the end of a rope where the group cannot verify if the rappelling rope has reached the bottom - and prevents the rappeller from falling off the strand if not paying attention.

The Figure 8 knot (and its variations) one that gets frequently in the sport, due to how often you are transitioning to/from rappels and clipping into things/people/anchors.

This is knot is easy to memorize and tie.

Everyone in your group should learn how to do this and know the variations of this knot.

Also, using the Figure 8 Knot, there is a way of joining (called a "bend") two ropes together, but it is called the *Figure-8 Bend*.

Pros:
- Larger and more secure than an overhand knot for stopping rope ends.
- Easy to tie, inspect, and untie.

Cons:
- Slightly bulkier than an overhand, potentially snagging in tight rope systems.

Caution:
- Ensure proper dressing to maintain its function as a stopper.
- The usage of this stopper knot by itself is in the "it depends" scenario.
- You would NEVER tie this on Class C canyons where there is an active water current.
- You may consider using the knot when you can't see if the rappelling rope has reached the bottom or not, and you would use it as a "stopper knot." Meaning, that if you were to reach the bottom of the rope (due to inattentiveness or other factors), you won't fall off the end of the rope. This knot would literally stop so you wouldn't do so.

Canyoneering Usage Examples:
- Used on the rappelling rope when you can't see if the rope has reached the bottom or not.
- Securing rope tails in belay systems or rappel backups.

Additional Reading:
- Wikipedia.org: "Figure-eight knot"

To begin, you will be working with one end of the rope.

(But the Figure 8 can be tied anywhere along the rope).

Next, make a loop on that rope.

(Below, I have the working end of the rope laying on top)

Take the working end of the rope from that loop you just made and go UNDER the rope as shown below.

Take the working end of the rope and go OVER one part of the loop and UNDER another part.

OVER

UNDER

Last, "dress the knot."

(Pull tightly on both sides of the knot to secure it.)

That's it!

Figure-8 Knot: On a Bight

The **Figure-8 On-A-Bight** is used in Canyoneering primarily for creating a "load carrying" loop. It is a safe knot to rappel on, to tie yourself into an anchor point, and to lower or raise people and gear.

To tie, simply make a bight on the rope followed by tying a Figure 8 knot.

Pros:
- Creates a secure loop for clipping into anchors or harnesses.
- Holds strong under load and is easy to untie afterward.

Cons:
- Bulky, which can be a challenge in systems requiring compact knots.

Caution:

- Always inspect for proper dressing to avoid weakening the knot.

Canyoneering Usage Examples:

- Creating a secure loop for connecting a rope to a carabiner when setting up a belay anchor or rappel system.
- Attaching personal safety tethers to anchors during canyon traverses or while waiting at rappel stations.

Additional Reading:

- CanyoneeringUSA.com: "Figure Eight on a Bight & Variations"
- Ropewiki.com: "Figure 8 (knot)"

Take any part of the rope and make a bight, as show below.

Take that bight and cross a part of the rope to form a loop, as shown below

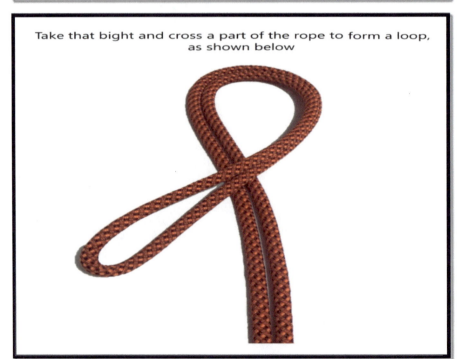

Take the bight end of the rope and do a half-wrap around the rope strands.

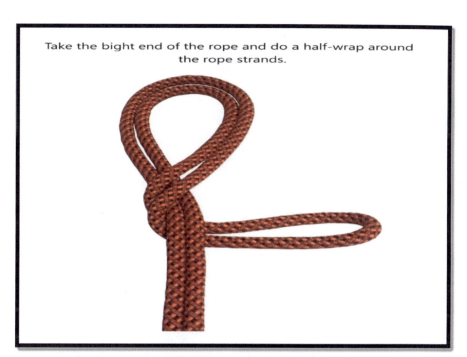

Next, enter the bight through the top of the loop...

...and pull the bight through the bottom of the loop.

"Dress the knot".
(Do this by pulling on both sides of the knot firmly).

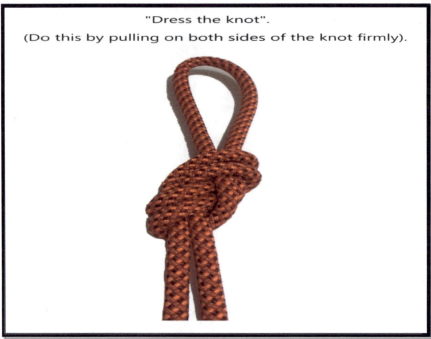

Rappelling on this could be dangerous!

Can you see the difference between THIS and a Figure 8 Bend?

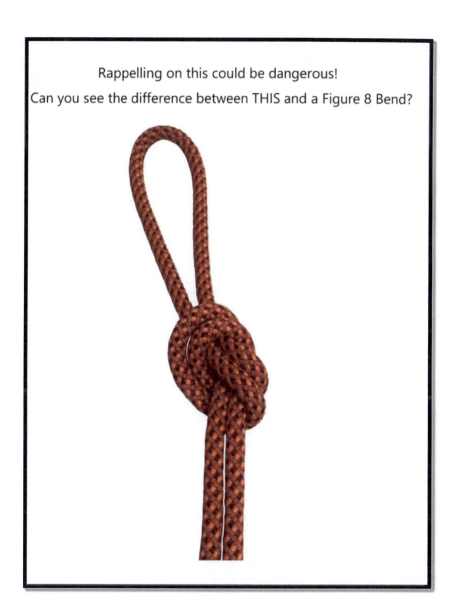

Figure-8 Knot: Follow-Through

The **Figure 8 Knot - Follow-through** is used in Canyoneering for creating a "load carrying" loop.

Once tied correctly, the follow-through versus the bight will allow you tie the Figure 8 know when the LOOP you are wanting to attach to is already there.

With this knot, you will be able to tie it into things such as harnesses, backpacks, anchors, and even people (like a kid who is too light to rappel).

NOTE - if you are LOWERING people, you will need to research into "belaying" people and need to find the best or appropriate way in doing so as it depends on the persons weight, the height of the rappel, how much rope you have, and what canyoneering descender devices you have with you.

Pros:
- Useful for tying loops around fixed objects like anchors or harnesses.
- Easy to inspect for proper alignment, ensuring safety under load.

Cons:
- More time-consuming to tie than a Figure 8 on a Bight.

Caution:
- Inspect alignment carefully to avoid compromising knot strength.

Canyoneering Usage Examples:
- Tying a loop around fixed objects like tree roots, boulders, or anchor rings for a secure rappel setup.
- Securing rope systems in areas where direct attachment to a structure is required, such as in multi-pitch canyon descents.

Additional Reading:
- DyeClan.com: "Figure 8 Follow Through"

The Figure 8 "follow-through" is simply a "Figure 8 on a bight" but instead allows you to tie the knot where there is ALREADY a loop or object in place.

IE.To tie it to a harness, carabiner, backpack, other loops to lower gear or people.

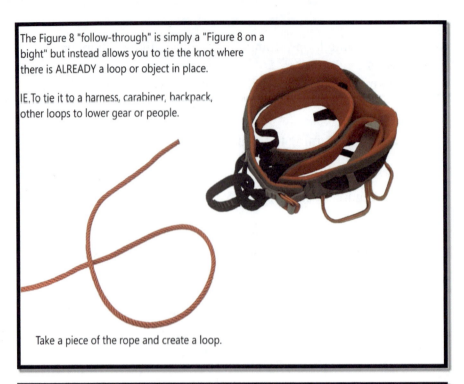

Take a piece of the rope and create a loop.

Once the loop is created, take the "working end" of the rope and go over the rope, as shown below.

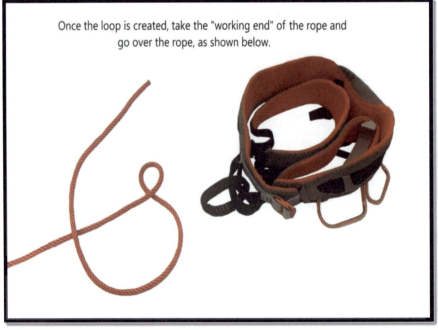

Next, put that end THROUGH the loop.

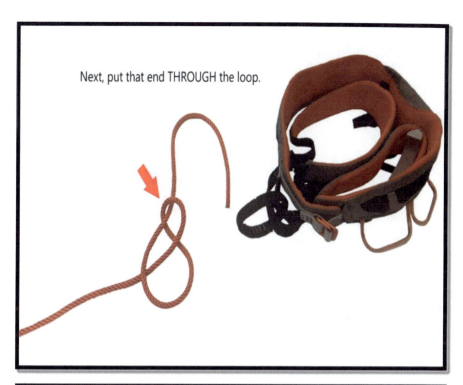

Next, take the strand that just went through the loop,
and put it through the harness (or carabiner, backpack loop, etc).

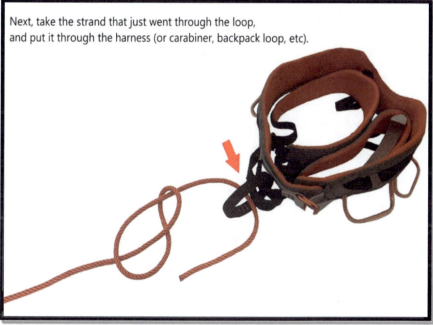

Take the rope strand and go back THROUGH the
loop you made earlier. This is called a "rethread" or
"rethreading the rope".

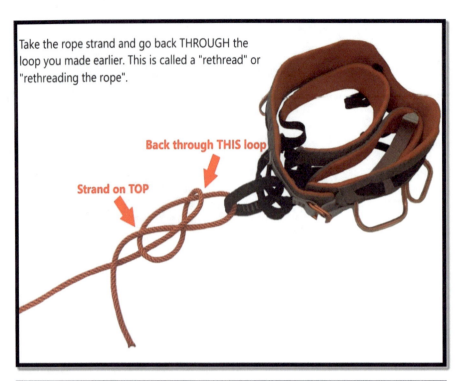

Back through THIS loop

Strand on TOP

Take that strand of rope and go under and through
the loop at the bottom (following the rope strand).
After, you will continue to rethread in reverse.

(You will only go through the belay loop once.)

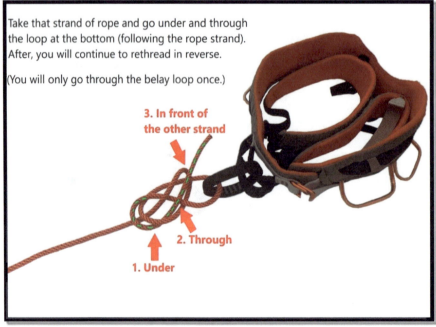

**3. In front of
the other strand**

2. Through

1. Under

Take that strand and continue the rethread in reverse. (Notice, how the rope did NOT go through the belay loop again on the harness.)

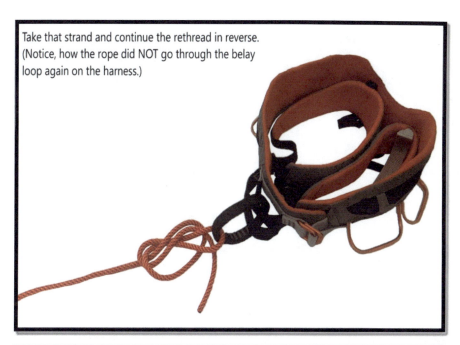

Take the working end and put it back through the loop farthest away from you.

Through the double loop

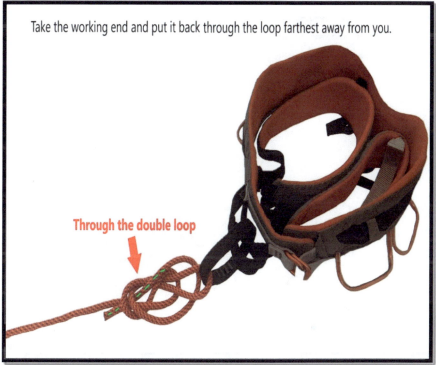

Here, the knot is "dressed" and forms the Figure 8 Knot.

Pull snugly on each rope strand surrounding the knot to ensure that the knot is secure.

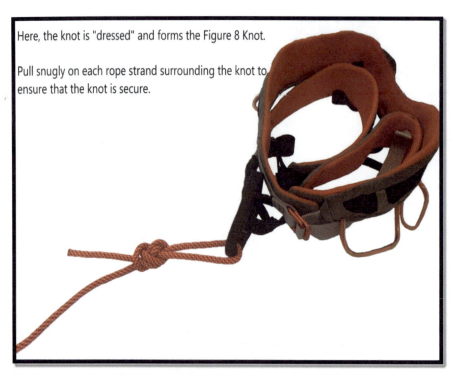

Here, the harness and knot are upside down to see the Figure 8 Knot from a different angle.

Clove Hitch/Triple Clove Hitch

Remember from our "Rope Terminology" learning module, that the word "hitch" means to tie a rope into an object. Why might you do that - tie a rope to an object? In canyoneering, we tie into a lot of "objects" so that we can rappel, build anchors, and even belay people.

The **Clove Hitch** is primarily used for forming the famous "biner (pronounced "bean-er") block".

This is used when we want to rappel single-strand (also called SRT (Single-Rope Technique) but we need to create a "block" so that we can retrieve our ropes when we touch the bottom. This allows us at the anchor point to rappel off one-side of the rope strand and NOT the other. You NEED to rappel off the blocked strand. If you rappel on the other strand, you fall all the way to ground with no resistance.

There have been a few accident reports of people becoming complacent, or they didn't know what they were doing, and did this exact same thing! One person is very lucky to survive especially as the person fell 90+ ft off a free-hang straight into the sand below. Others have not been so lucky and ended up losing their lives. YOU MUST pay attention, every time, at every rappel, to make sure that everyone is rappelling on the correct strand of the rope.

There have been some reports of the clove hitch moving or unraveling due to an incorrect tying, using extreme force, in addition to not dressing the knot, and not subsequently "testing" (or loading the rappel) before a person rappels.

Since those reports have come out, the canyoneering community has now suggested moving to what's called the **"Triple-Clove Hitch"**. This will ensure that knot cannot come undone, all while keeping it still easy to tie. All you add is another loop to the standard clove hitch with the carabiner going through all 3 loops.

Pros:
- Easy to tie/untie.
- Can be tied with one hand.

Cons:
- Does not allow for a lowering method if the rappeller was to become stuck for whatever reason. This is where having a second rappelling rope would be crucial.

Caution:
- After hearing a report of the clove hitch coming undone (because it wasn't dressed properly), the community in response to keep beginners safer are recommending the "Triple Clove". This is tied by simply adding one more loop (or twist) in the rope and having the carabiner go through all three loops.
- Avoid use on slick or stiff ropes without additional security (such as tying a "triple clove hitch")

Canyoneering Usage Examples:
- Use it to set up a block system rappel
- Quickly attaching a rope to a carabiner when creating a temporary anchor system

Additional Reading:
- CanyoneeringUSA.com: "Biner Blocks and Pull Cord Techniques for Backcountry Canyoneering"

To begin, you will be working with one end of the rope

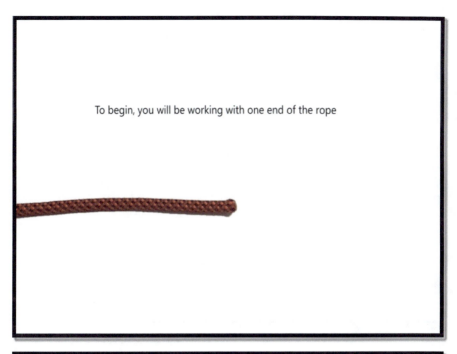

Next, make a loop about a foot (12 inches) away from the end of the rope.

(I just take a few inches of the rope and do one counter- clockwise, 180-degree twist on the rope).

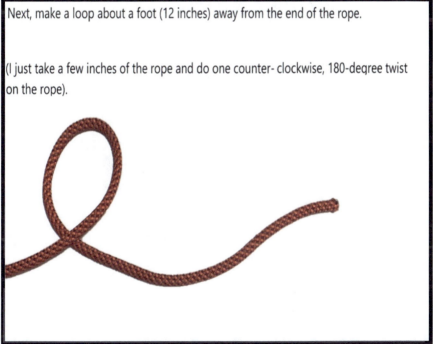

Make another loop on the rope, using the same technique as you did on the first loop.

I do two counter-clockwise, 180-degree twists of the rope to get what you see below.

Take the right loop and lay it on top of the left loop.

(Don't take it underneath!)

Take a carabiner and have it go through both loops.

NOTE Be sure to "lock" (or twist) the carabiner closed after going through both loops.

"Dress the knot".

In other words, pull on both strands on either side of the knot to make it snug against the carabiner.

This is the finished result. Notice that there is about one-foot (12 inches) of tail remaining.

This is a different angle of the Clove Hitch

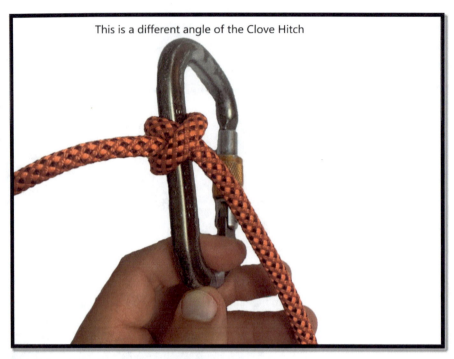

The Clove Hitch should be located on the "spine" of the carabiner.

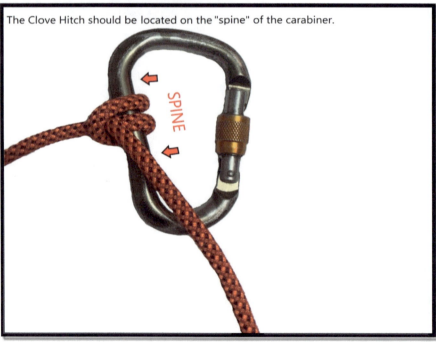

How to Tie TRIPLE CLOVE HITCH

TRIPLE-CLOVE TECHNIQUE

In addition to the two loops you made for the original Clove Hitch, you will be adding ONE MORE loop for the Triple-Clove Hitch.

Take the middle loop and lay it on top of the left loop. Then take the right loop and lay it on the top.

Take a carabiner and put it through all 3 loops.

"Dress the knot".

Pull snug on either side of the knot in both directions.

This is what it should look like when it is finished.

Another angle of the Triple-Clove Hitch

This what it should like when you are done.

NOTE Be sure to "lock" off the carabiner when finished.

Munter Hitch

The **Munter Hitch** is another essential knot to know as it can provide a way to rappel down a rope in the event you lose or drop your "rappel device". Example: You are unhooking your descender device from the previous rappel and drop it in a pool of water and it's too muddy to find it; or you when you are connecting to the rope, your descender falls off the cliff. How will you continue through the canyon now? If there aren't any more rappels, you are lucky. How will you rappel? Enter the Munter Hitch.)

IMPORTANT NOTE - the Munter Hitch should never be used a primary way of rappelling. It puts incredible force and wear and tear on the rope. Some claim that it destroys the rope with extended usage. This is to be used essentially for emergencies, only. Losing your descender device in a slot canyon is more common than one might think. (I have lost one in pothole and another off a cliff while connecting into the rope.)

This is an easy knot to tie and is just a slight variation from the clove hitch. But instead of putting the loop on top of the other loop to make the clove-hitch, you just put the two loops face-to-face and have the carabiner got through both loops. That's it.

Pros:
- Provides a way to rappel when there is no descender/rappel device (either with a carabiner or not).
- Simple to learn and use in emergencies.

Cons:
- If not paying close attention, it can get confused with the Clove Hitch.
- Causes significant rope twisting and sheath damage with repeated use.
- Offers less friction control than dedicated devices.

Caution:
- Reserve for emergencies; avoid prolonged use to prevent excessive rope wear and rope damage.

Canyoneering Usage Examples:
- Emergency rappelling when a device like a descender device is unavailable (dropped in a pothole, forgotten or misplaced, etc.)
- Can belay a partner with minimal equipment during rescue or unexpected scenarios.

Additional Reading:
- Canyoneering.net: "Need-To-Know Canyon Knots"
- Wikipedia.org: "Munter hitch"
- Dyeclan.com: "Munter Hitch (Italian Hitch)"
- RopeWiki.com: "Munter hitch"

Start off as if you were tying a clove-hitch

Don't put the loop on top of the other loop,
but instead have them face-to-face

Here the two loops (from the clove-hitch formation) are face-to-face

People call this "kissing each other"

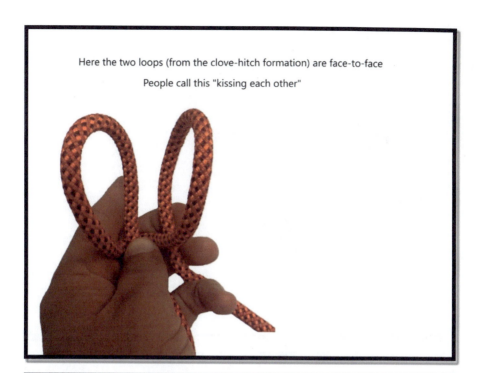

The carabiner goes through both loops
(with the two loops on the "spine" of the carabiner)

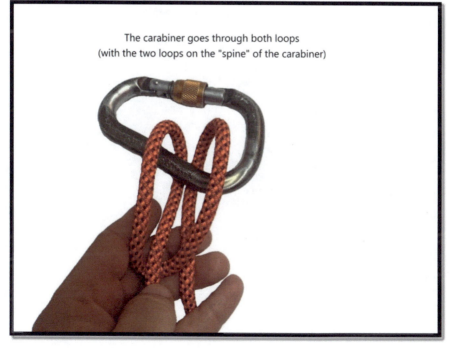

Dress the knot

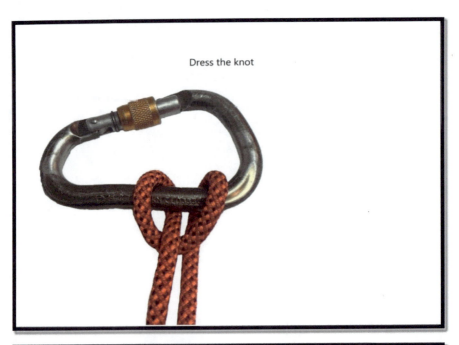

(This is a side-angle of the Munter)

Once it is dressed, you are good go!

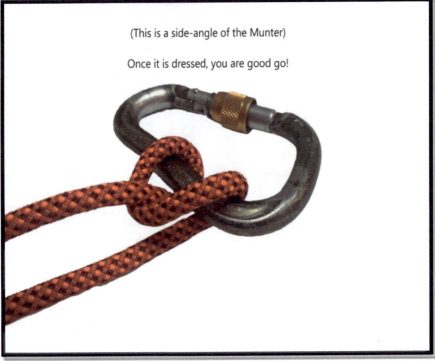

Girth Hitch

The **Girth Hitch** is used in Canyoneering to tie the knot to an object. Most of the applications I have seen this used is when canyoneers use a P.A.S (Personal Anchor System) to tie it to their harness.

The reason why you would use this one, is that is incredible easy to tie, and it saves the person from using a carabiner on one side. The other side will need a carabiner so that it can clip into things. Especially when used in "fall protection" scenarios.

This is *NOT* used for rappelling but rather to attach a rope to an object (and save a carabiner in the process), even one handed!

The Girth Hitch is also how you form part of the Prussik knot.

Pros:
- Efficient for attaching loops to anchors or other objects (such as your PAS to the rappelling anchor).
- Easy to tie and untie, making it a practical choice for quick setups.

Cons:
- Reduces sling strength significantly, sometimes up to 50% (but strong enough to keep a person from falling at the anchor point).
- Susceptible to failure under dynamic loads.

Caution:
- Don't use this hitch in rescue scenarios. Use other stronger knots in those cases.

Canyoneering Usage Examples:

- Attaching slings to harnesses, rappel devices, or anchors in a quick way.
- Connecting personal tethers or safety lanyards to an anchor during belay transitions or rappel preparation.

Additional Resources:
- Canyoneering.net: "Need-To-Know Canyon Knots"
- NetKnots.com: "Girth Hitch - How to tie a Girth Hitch"
- Dyeclan.com: "Girth Hitch (Cow Hitch, Lark's Head)"
- Wikipedia.org: "Cow Hitch"

Make a bight in the rope

Take the bight and pull the two rope strands through it.

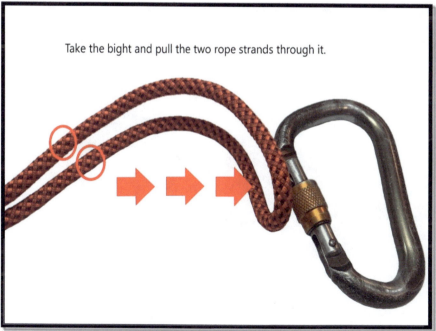

Another angle of the bight and pulling the two strands through it.

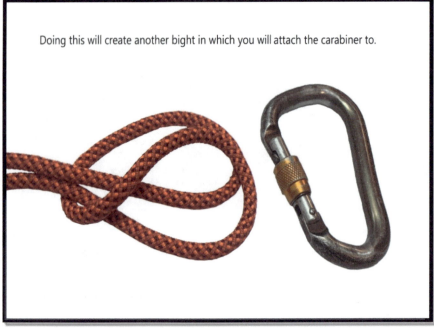

Doing this will create another bight in which you will attach the carabiner to.

The carabiner is now attached.

"Dress the knot"
(Pull on the two strands so it is snug against the carabiner)

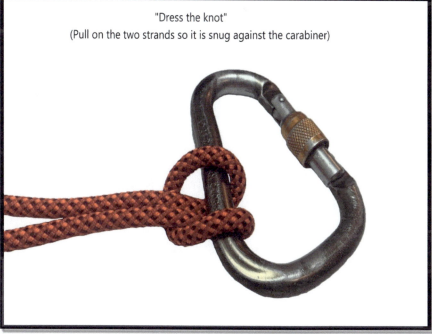

An upside-down view of the knot.

Stone Hitch

Part of me hesitates to call the **Stone Hitch** an essential knot, but a larger part believes its underrated and deserves more recognition. I love this knot not only because it's easy to tie, but more importantly, because it isolates both strands of the rope.

This means one person can rappel using SRT (Single Rope Technique) independently from the other person. Unlike other knots, which don't isolate the strands, this allows two people to rappel simultaneously without affecting each other. Their weight, size, or technique (they finish rappelling before or after you) won't impact the other person - for example, whether one person weighs 300 pounds and the other weighs 60 pounds, they remain unaffected.

The primary use of this knot in canyoneering is for sequencing, where is significantly speeds up rappels. This is especially valuable in canyons with numerous rappels, when managing large groups, or with a mix of beginners and experts. Practiced effectively, the Stone Hitch can save critical daylight, addressing one of the biggest timewasters in canyoneering.

Pros:
- Allows for two people at the same time to rappel independently of each other.
- Allows for releasable toggles to be used (such as FiddleStick/Smooth Operator/etc.)
- In conjunction with other practices, this is used in "Ghosting" techniques for Canyoneering.

Cons:
- Must have an extra carabiner (or releasable toggle) to use.
- Cannot be used to lower stuck rappellers.

Caution:
- This hitch HAS to be untied before the last rappeller goes! If you don't, you will need to ASCEND the rope (hopefully you have the experience!) and untie it. Otherwise, you are stuck!
- Verify knot dressing/integrity before starting a rappel.

Canyoneering Usage Examples:
- Isolating rappel strands for group descents, allowing simultaneous rappelling on either strand of the rope (regardless of other factors such as person's weight, descender device, whether they are at the top or finished the rappel)
- Setting up a system for faster group efficiency when managing multiple rappellers in a canyon.
- Overlap rappellers getting on the rappel and getting off the rappel, which can speed the total descent time.

Additional Reading:
- CanyoneeringUSA.com: "The Stone Knot (aka Stein Knot): A Canyoneering Secret Weapon"
- Ropewiki.com: "Stone knot"
- DyeClan.com: "Stone Knot (Stein Knot)"

First, create a bight in the rope strands.

About a foot from the end of the bight, create a loop with the strands ON TOP.

ROPE STRANDS ON TOP

Bring the loop up from the bottom and lay it on top of the rope
Essentially you are folding the loop over itself.

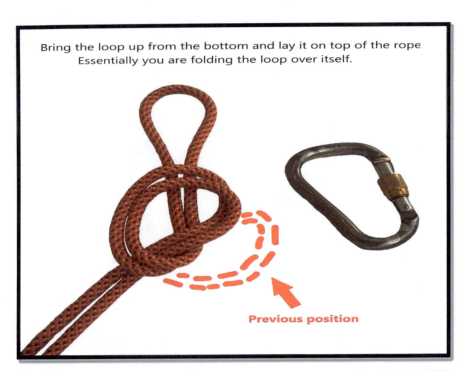

Previous position

Pull the two strands of rope towards YOU to create a bight.

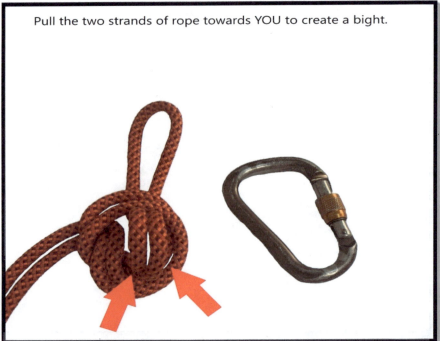

Attach the carabiner to the bight.
Finally, "Dress the knot".
WARNING - IF YOU REMOVE THE CARABINER, the KNOT FAILS!!

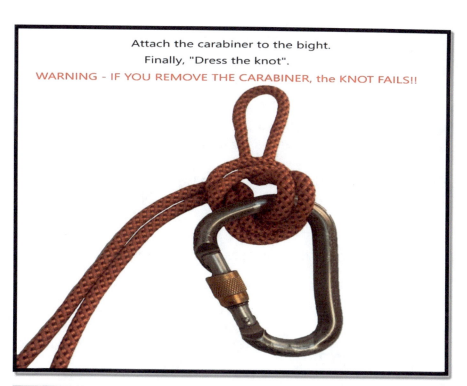

As a safety precaution, attach the carabiner through the bight at top.

This is to prevent the knot from untieing itself on its own.

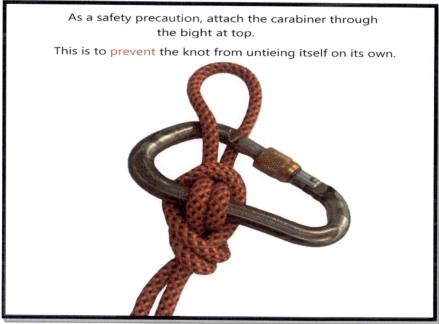

European Death Knot (EDK)

Also called: "Flat Overhand Knot", "Offset Overhand Bend", "Thumb Knot", "Thumb Bend". Please call it the **E.D.K.** as the other names are not known in the Canyoneering universe.

The E.D.K. is a very quick way of tying two ropes together. This is listed here for only retrieving your rappel rope; NOT rappelling on. BIG difference!

It does not matter that the two ropes are not the same thickness.

The **IMPORTANT** thing is that you tie a minimum of *two* over-hand knots (also called "double EDK" or "double stacked") with a maximum of *three* (also called "triple EDK" or "triple-stacked"). That's all it is...two or three overhand knots using the two ropes.

Pros:

- Easy to remember (just three overhand knots, next to each other)
- Quickly connects two ropes (of the same diameter or not) to retrieve your rappel rope.

Cons:

- Although simple, if tied incorrectly, it can lead to grave bodily harm and death.
- If rigged incorrectly to rappel on, the knot can "capsize" (or "roll").
- NEVER USED for rappelling in canyoneering.

Caution:

- Leave 12 inches (extreme minimum) to 24 inches of tail.
- Do NOT tie the EDK on webbing! It will fail when loaded over 1100 lb. (The Water Knot fails over 2000 lb.)
- Do NOT use the EDK on very stiff ropes (IE brand new).
- On brand new ropes, use a more secure knot such as the Double-Fisherman Bend.

Canyoneering Usage Examples:

- **Scenario**: the tallest rappel in a canyon is 90 ft. You bring a 100-foot 9 mm rope to rappel on, and you also bring a 100-foot 6 mm pull-cord to retrieve your 9 mm. When you are setting up your rigging, one way is to use an EDK knot on both ropes so that you would use the 6 mm rope as a pull-cord to retrieve the 9 mm rappel rope.

Additional Reading:

- Wikipedia.org: "Offset Overhand Bend"
- YouTube: "Canyons & Crags - "Flat Overhand Knot - the European Death Knot""
- Canyoneering.net: "EDK in Webbing?"
- CanyoneeringUSA.com: "How to Tie Two Ropes Together"

Lay two strands of rope side-by-side of each other.

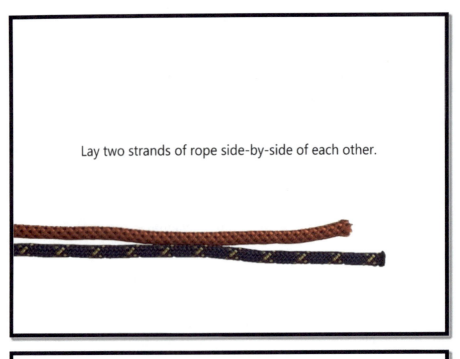

It's IMPORTANT to leave about 12 inches (24" is preferred) of tail from both ropes.

Tie an Overhand Knot using both strands.

While keeping the end of the rope longer than 12" to the first Overhand knot, tie a second Overhand knot.

1st Overhand Knot

2nd Overhand Knot

Make one more Overhand knot for a total of 3.
Afterwards, "Dress the Knot".

That's it!

1st Overhand Knot

2nd Overhand Knot

3rd Overhand Knot

Double (or Triple)-Fisherman Bend

The **Double-Fisherman Bend**, which in rope nomenclature means to "join" two ropes together.

It is a popular, secure (safe) load bearing, knot that would be safe to rappel on. In contrast and for re-emphasis, the EDK knot is a simple and easy way to join two ropes together but is NOT safe to rappel on. The Double-Fisherman Bend is safe and secure to rappel on.

It should be noted that ropes made with Technora or Dyneema can be "slick" (which means you will have less friction) to rappel on and likewise goes with this knot, to add another margin of safety, a Triple-Fisherman Bend is recommended if you use ropes made with those components.

To tie, you will lay two rope ends next to each other and wrap around one rope twice and then using the other rope to wrap around it twice, followed by going through those wraps and pulling tightly. Then pull on both ropes so that the knots are against each other.

Note: To do a Triple-Fisherman Bend, instead of wrapping the rope twice, you would do it three times.

Pros:
- One of the most secure knots for joining two ropes together, with the same rope thickness or not (a 9 mm and 9 mm, and 8 mm and 11 mm, etc.)
- The knot tightens under load, making it very unlikely to fail.

Cons:
- Quite difficult to untie, especially once loaded. a bulky knot and must be considered if the canyon constricts or narrows and the knot is unable to go over the rappel edge, etc.

Caution:
- Triple-Fisherman Bend is recommended if you use ropes made with Technora or Dyneema.

Canyoneering Usage Examples:
- Securing two ropes together when strength and durability are the top priorities, such as during heavy-load rappels.
- Creating strong loops in cordage for prusiks or other friction hitches used in rescue scenarios.

Additional Reading:
- Wikipedia.org: "Double fisherman's knot"
- DyeClan.com: "Double Fisherman's Bend (Grapevine Knot)"
- CanyoneeringUSA.com: "How to Tie Two Ropes Together"
- NetKnots.com: "Double Fisherman's Knot"

Lay the two ropes side-by-side with the rope ends opposite of each other.

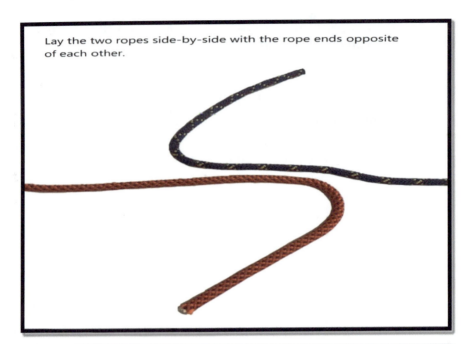

Start with either rope strand and do a wrap around the other rope strand, working from an outside to inward direction.

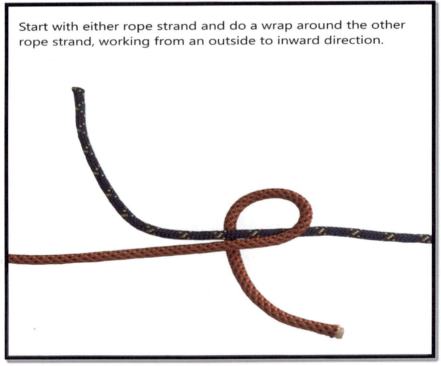

Do another (second) wrap around both rope strands.

The second wrap is why its called a "double" fisherman.

Working in this direction

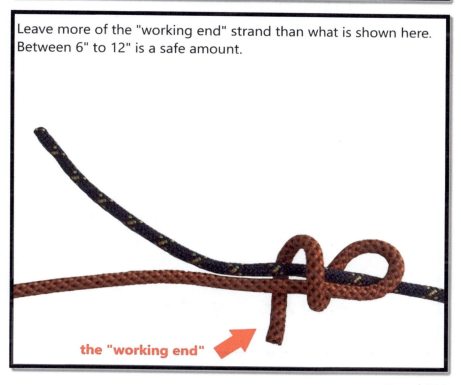

Leave more of the "working end" strand than what is shown here. Between 6" to 12" is a safe amount.

the "working end"

After the second wrap is complete, take that working end and go through both loops, as shown below.

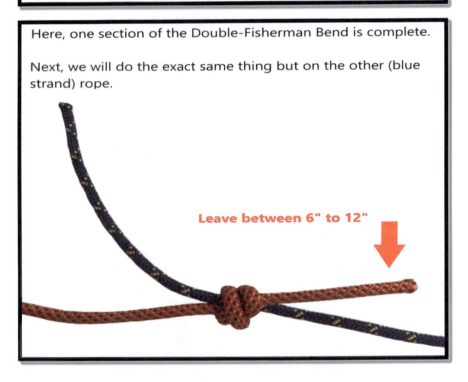

the "working end" goes through the two loops THIS direction (away from the inside)

Here, one section of the Double-Fisherman Bend is complete.

Next, we will do the exact same thing but on the other (blue strand) rope.

Leave between 6" to 12"

Take the other (blue) strand of rope and do a wrap around the other (red) rope. Just like before, you will be working from the outside-towards-the-inside direction.

Here, one wrap around the red rope is complete. We will next do another wrap around the red rope working from the outside in.

Working in this direction

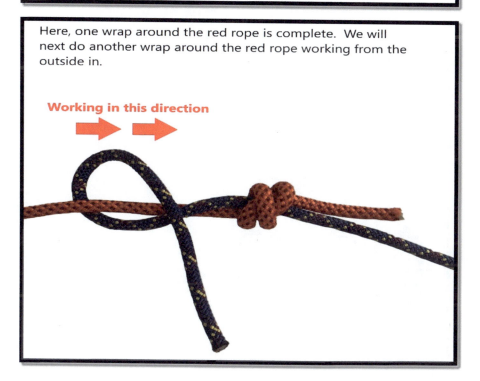

Almost there; wrapping around the red rope a second time.

Two wraps are now done and for the next step we will take the blue strand and put it back through both loops working from the inside out.

Here, the blue strand has gone through both loops.

Be sure to "dress" the knot by pulling tight on either side of the knot.

The knot will move freely on both ropes strands. This is normal.

The Double-Fisherman Bend works safely by having each knot pull against each other.

Again, make sure that the tail end of both rope strands are between 6" to 12" in length.

Here, the Bend is in its completed form with both knots pulling against each other.

Pull on both rope strands to dress the Bend completely.

Figure-8 Bend

A Figure-8 Bend is a strong, secure knot in JOINING two ropes together. Remember that the word "bend" in rope terminology means to join.

Pros:
- Easier to untie than the Double Fisherman's Bend.
- Strong and reliable for ropes of the same diameter.

Cons:

- While sufficient for knot security for joining two ropes together and even rappelling on them, the double-fisherman is "more" secure as it becomes tighter.
- Not ideal for ropes with significant diameter differences or stiffness.

Caution:
- Always inspect the knot for proper dressing and tensioning.

Canyoneering Usage Examples:
- Joining two ropes for a rappel setup in situations where the ropes are the same diameter and flexibility
- Tying together shorter rope segments for temporary canyoneering applications

Additional Reading:
- Wikipedia.org: "Flemish Bend"
- NetKnots.com: "Flemish Bend - How to Tie"

To create the Figure 8 Bend ("Bend" is the terminology for joining two ropes), you will be working with two different rope ends (as shown below).

With one end of the rope, create a loop.

After creating the loop, go underneath the strand

Take the strand and go UNDER (or through) the loop

through the loop

Take the strand through the loop on the red rope, as shown below.

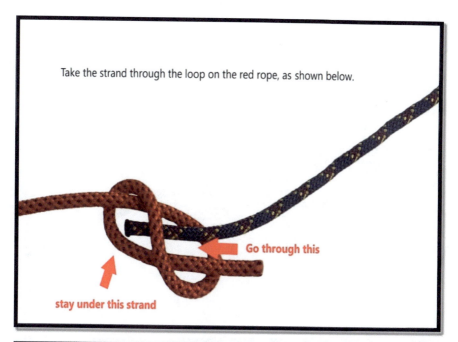

Go through this

stay under this strand

Take the strand and put it through the loop on the red rope.

This loop

Put the blue strand through the loop on the red rope, as shown below.

Take the strand and bring it to the front of the right loop.

Bring it in front of the loop

Next, put the strand first through though loop on the red rope,
followed by the loop on the blue rope, as shown below.

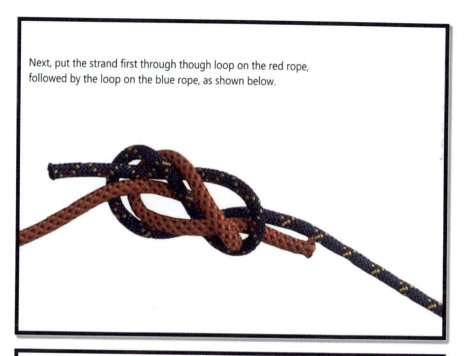

"Dress the knot"
(Pull both strands firmly on either side of the knot to make the knot snug against each other).

Made in United States
Troutdale, OR
04/21/2025